IRELAND'S COUNTY HIGH POINTS

A Walking Guide

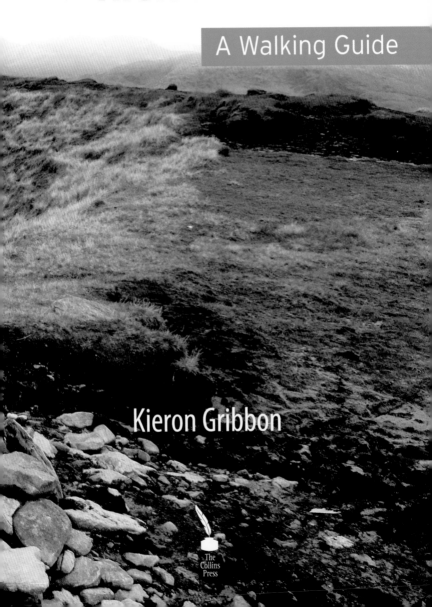

Kieron Gribbon

The
Collins
Press

First published in 2012 by
The Collins Press
West Link Park
Doughcloyne
Wilton
Cork

British Library Cataloguing in Publication data
Gribbon, Kieron.
Ireland's county high points : a walking guide.
1. Walking—Ireland—Guidebooks. 2. Ireland—Altitudes.
3. Ireland—Guidebooks.
I. Title
796.5'1'09415-dc23

ISBN-13: 9781848891401

Design & typesetting by Fairways Design

Typeset in Avenir

Printed in the Czech Republic by Finidr

All photos and maps in this book have been personally created by the author.

Contents

Leinster

Broken trig pillar marking the County High Point of Galway at Benbaun summit

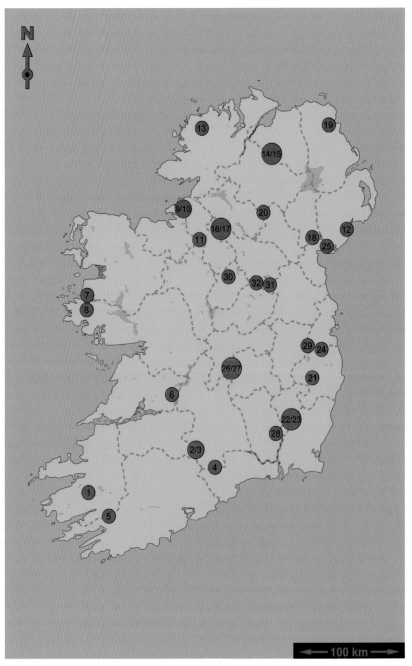

County High Point walk locations. Numbers indicate the relevant chapters for each walk.

Acknowledgements

During the ten months in which I walked every County High Point (CHP) for this book, I shared the journey with some of the most special people in my life. I thank my wife, Gráinne, who is by now almost halfway through her own CHP challenge – I plan to revisit with her those high points that remain on her 'to do' list. An extra thank-you to her also for the patience, understanding and strength she has shown throughout the whole process. I thank John – my father-in-law and good friend – who has also bagged a few CHPs with me along the way. Thanks to Fionnuala and Brian for joining me in the mountains and for their support. My sincere appreciation goes to the Northern Ireland Young Walkers walking club, with whom I have climbed several CHPs in Ireland – and beyond – since 2006.

A special thank-you to my parents, Brendan and Rosemarie, for making me the person I am today and for their words of encouragement during the writing of this book and throughout my life.

I thank all the very helpful and talented people throughout Ireland who assisted me by answering the queries I posed while researching this book. These include staff members in various local councils, tourism and outdoor sports bodies, OSi, OSNI, and accommodation providers throughout Ireland.

Thank you to The Collins Press for believing in this project and to Fairways Design for their part in the creation of this book.

Last, but by no means least: on behalf of all walkers with an appreciation for the countryside and for those who live and work in it, I would like to thank all landowners and primary land users who happily share with us these beautiful and special places in Ireland. In particular, a thank-you from me to the landowners with whom I have spoken in the field. Their knowledge of the local mountains and hills is second to none, and cannot be found in any guidebook.

Kieron Gribbon

Introduction

Whether you are a leisurely rambler or a serious mountaineer, there is a good chance you will have already visited – or plan to visit – at least one of Ireland's County High Points. While this special set of Irish hills and mountains continues to attract more and more visitors each year, they have never before had a walking guidebook exclusively devoted to them – until now. *Ireland's County High Points – A Walking Guide* explains, in a county-by-county format, everything you need to know as a walker before setting out on your County High Point quests. Each county-focused chapter contains a brief county profile, detailed walking routes, and easy-to-read indicative maps which have all been personally created by the author himself. Details of any notable hazards and access restrictions are also highlighted where they occur. This definitive guide to Ireland's County High Points is based entirely on on-site research combined with detailed desk-study investigation, and dispels any commonly believed myths that may have previously lingered over certain County High Point locations.

The Counties of Ireland: A Brief History

For the purposes of this book, the counties of Ireland are the thirty-two traditional counties which cover the Republic of Ireland and Northern Ireland, including all of their jurisdictional offshore islands – from hereon referred to collectively as Ireland. The county boundaries referred to throughout this book are consistent with those marked on the most recent editions of 1:50,000 scale maps published by the Ordnance Survey Ireland (OSi) and the Ordnance Survey of Northern Ireland (OSNI).

The evolution of the county boundaries was a long process which started in the twelfth century following the Norman invasion. They were first introduced as shires under English rule, although some shire boundaries corresponded with those of already-established Irish clan territories. There have been significant revisions down the centuries, but many sections of those original shire and clan boundaries still remain part of today's county system.

Between the thirteenth and seventeenth centuries, counties merged and split. Some were transferred back and forth between the four provinces of Ulster, Munster, Leinster and Connacht (and the former fifth province of Mide). By the early seventeenth century, the county boundaries had largely become what they are today. Several enclaves still existed remotely outside the county they were part of, completely surrounded by neighbouring counties. In the mid-nineteenth century, those enclaves were absorbed into their surrounding counties to create the 'traditional' arrangement that is still in use today.

Ireland remained under British rule until Partition in 1921, when independence was granted to the twenty-six counties now known as the Republic of Ireland. Britain retained control over the six Northern Ireland counties, which continue to form part of the United Kingdom.

Irish local government was, for a long time, based on the modern-day county system. In 1973, the six counties of Northern Ireland ceased to be recognised in this capacity, being replaced by twenty-six smaller district, borough and city councils. The layout of Northern Ireland's local council areas is currently being reviewed. In the Republic of Ireland, most present-day county council boundaries correspond with those of the traditional counties. Two counties in the Republic (Dublin and Tipperary) have been split into smaller county-level council areas, and five city councils have also been created. In all, the Republic has thirty-four county-level council areas.

The all-Ireland and provincial championships governed by the Gaelic Athletic Association are largely based on the traditional county system, and players of the games demonstrate total commitment to their county – as do their loyal and proud supporters. And, of course, the thirty-two traditional counties are important to those of us who seek out the County High Points.

What is a County High Point?

A County High Point is, quite simply, the point on the surface of a particular county which is higher than every other point in that same county. Often referred to as a County Top or County Peak, it is located either directly on or within the respective county's boundaries. From here on, the abbreviation CHP will be used in place of 'County High Point'.

A CHP may be an unmarked location, but is often marked by an Ordnance Survey triangulation station (e.g. a trig pillar) or a stone cairn. Where it is marked by a trig pillar, the top of the pillar is the CHP. If it is marked by a loosely constructed stone cairn, the CHP is located at natural ground level beneath the cairn. However, if the stones in the cairn are held firmly in place within a soil matrix and cannot be easily moved, the top of the cairn is the CHP. Physically touching the top of a relevant trig pillar or stone cairn qualifies as having visited a CHP. In County Down, there is a choice of two CHP locations at Slieve Donard summit – a roof-mounted trig pillar or a large stone cairn. Touching the top of either qualifies, although the dedicated high-pointer will probably want to do both – just to be sure. The recommended option, however, is the cairn, even though the trig pillar is higher, purely for safety reasons. The CHP of Kerry is marked by the base of a large metal cross at Carrauntoohil summit – touching this cross qualifies. Unmarked CHPs are more difficult to pinpoint. These locations are described in this book, and GPS coordinates (to an accuracy of 10m) will guide you close to the spot. From here, you must make an on-site assessment and decide if you are at the CHP. Judging this exact spot will vary from person to person, so standing within 10m of an unmarked CHP qualifies. The tops of trees, telecommunications masts, pylons, poles and wind turbines do not count as they cannot be accessed safely.

There are in total thirty-one locations in Ireland which fulfil the above CHP criteria. These are located on twenty-six mountains and hills throughout the thirty-two counties of Ireland. In addition to these, a further fifteen locations have been identified in this book – each being the highest unshared summit in a county whose CHP is located on a shared summit or on a slope.

At the other end of the scale, a County Low Point is the point in a particular county which is lower than every other point in that same county. For a coastal county, the entire length of its coastline at sea level represents the County Low Point. For landlocked counties, the County Low Point can generally be found where a particular river flows across a boundary and into a neighbouring county. It may also be a portion of a lake.

Why visit Ireland's County High Points?

Here are a few reasons why people choose to visit one, some, or all of Ireland's CHPs:

- As part of a challenge (see Appendix)
- To visit the CHP of one's home county
- 360° views

Walking Ireland's County High Points

Route Specific Information

Time

Time ranges are stated throughout this book for each route detailed. These time ranges are based on slow and fast walking paces and have been calculated by considering the following set of variables: walking speeds; total distance; total ascent; terrain covered; and an allowance for stops.

1. Slow – walking pace of 18 minutes per kilometre. Additional 10 minutes per 100m ascent. Ten-minute stop added for each hour of walking time. Additional stops have not been factored in.

2. Fast – walking pace of 12 minutes per kilometre. Additional 10 minutes per 100m ascent. No allowance made for stops.

Grading

Grading of routes in this book has been based on length of route, type of terrain, total ascent and steepness of ascent. Routes are graded as follows:

1. Easy – clear tracks on even terrain. Less than 200m of ascent with no steep sections. Basic navigational skills useful but unlikely to be required.

2. Moderate – hilly and/or boggy terrain. Mainly on well-defined paths, although may not be obvious in some places. More than 200m of ascent, possibly with some short, steep sections. Basic navigational skills required, especially in mist and rain.

3. Challenging – mountainous and/or boggy terrain. Some well-defined paths, although likely to be unclear in places. More than 500m of ascent, including some steep sections. Well-practised navigational skills essential, especially in mist and rain. Average level of fitness required. Should only be attempted by well-equipped and experienced walkers if undertaken during wintry conditions.

4. Demanding – treacherous mountainous terrain requiring the crossing of intimidating ridges – a good head for heights is required. More than 800m of ascent, including some steep sections and scrambling. No path in places. Well-practised navigational skills essential, especially in mist and rain. High level of fitness required. Potentially a winter mountaineering expedition in snowy conditions – only to be attempted by well-equipped and highly experienced winter mountaineers during wintry conditions.

Land Ownership and Access Restrictions

Many of Ireland's CHPs – and the walking routes described in this book – occur on privately owned land which is used for agricultural purposes. Others occur on land owned or used by Coillte, Forest Service of Northern Ireland, RTÉ NL, Northern Ireland Water, the National Trust, the Department of Defence, and wind-farm operators.

Public access is permitted to the majority of the CHPs. This is largely due to the goodwill of landowners who understand and appreciate why walkers are drawn to these special places. There are, however, a couple of known (or suspected) exceptions mentioned in relevant walk descriptions. Access-restriction categories used in this book are:

1. **None –** unlimited access permitted along described route.
2. **None identified –** no access restrictions identified along described route. Unlimited access cannot be guaranteed as possible unmarked restrictions may exist. Walkers following any of the 'None identified' routes described in this book do so by their own choice and at their own risk. Walkers are advised to leave, without protest, any property if instructed to do so by the landowner.
3. **RTÉ NL access road –** walkers are advised to telephone the RTÉ NL Network Monitoring Centre (NMC) to request permission before embarking along any RTÉ NL access road. The NMC telephone number is 01 208 2259 – lines are staffed on weekdays between 7:00 a.m. and 12:00 midnight, and at weekends between 8:00 a.m. and 10:00 p.m. Also, check www.rtenl.ie for possible access restrictions in place due to maintenance work.
4. **Other identified access issues**

Countryside Etiquette

When in the countryside, use your common sense and display good manners at all times. This makes the countryside a pleasanter place to be and helps maintain good relationships between walkers, landowners and other land users.

Leave No Trace: self explanatory

Livestock and Dogs: never take a dog into an environment where livestock are likely to be encountered at close distance.

Stiles, Gates and Fences: before attempting to cross a fence, look for a stile to use. If there is none, look for a gate. Leave gates as you find them and do not damage any fences or gates if you decide to climb over.

Parking: where possible, leave your car in an official car park or roadside parking spot. If there is none available, park with consideration. Parking options are suggested in each walk description.

Say 'Hello'.

About This Book

For the purposes of this book, the thirty-two traditional counties of Ireland have been ranked from that with the highest CHP (i.e. Kerry = 1) to that with the lowest (i.e. Westmeath = 32). Where two counties share a CHP, that with the lower County Low Point is ranked higher as it has the greatest overall height range. In this book, a county is classed as being coastal if part of its perimeter is formed by an obvious sea coastline and/or a tidal inlet wider than 1km. Where two such counties share a CHP, the one with the longer coastal boundary is ranked higher.

The Irish county height rankings are:

Kerry (1); Wicklow (2); Limerick (3); Tipperary (4); Down (5); Mayo (6); Wexford (7); Carlow (8); Waterford (9); Dublin (10); Donegal (11); Galway (12); Cork (13); Derry (14); Tyrone (15); Fermanagh (16); Cavan (17); Sligo (18); Leitrim (19); Louth (20); Armagh (21); Antrim (22); Clare (23); Laois (24); Offaly (25); Kilkenny (26); Roscommon (27); Kildare (28); Monaghan (29); Longford (30); Meath (31); Westmeath (32).

By taking the average ranking of the counties in each of the four provinces, the provinces can be ranked in the following order:

Munster (1); Connacht (2); Ulster (3); Leinster (4).

Therefore, the layout of this book has been based initially on the ranking positions of the four provinces to establish the four main sections. Each of these provincial sections is further divided into chapters based on the ranking positions of that province's constituent counties. Each chapter focuses on a specific county and its CHP.

SUMMITS		WALKING	
▲	County High Point	▬▬▬	Walking route
▲	Other prominent summit or neighbouring CHP	▬ ▬	Alternative route
		– –	Path
RELIEF		c = = = = ᴐ	Track
		–––––––	Prominent fence
		——	Prominent wall
	1,000m	▪	Notable building
	750m		Woodland
	500m	///	Possible soft ground
	250m	**DRIVING**	
–––––	Contours (50m intervals)		Suggested inter-walk driving routes for CHP challenges
▲	Spot height (in metres)	=[M1]=	Motorway
GENERAL		=[N1]=	Major road
– – – – –	County boundary	=[B8]=	Medium road
–––––	River or stream	——	Minor road
	Lake or lough	④	Motorway junction
	Built-up area	◇T	Motorway toll plaza
●	City, town or village	◇S	Motorway service area
✈	Airport	P	Official car park
⛴	Ferry port	P	Roadside parking spot

Map symbols used in this book

The summit of Benbaun – County High Point of Galway

MUNSTER

Covering the southwestern quarter of Ireland, the province of Munster comprises the six counties of Kerry, Limerick, Tipperary, Waterford, Cork and Clare. With an area of 24,229km^2, Munster is the largest of Ireland's four provinces. Many of Ireland's highest mountain summits are in Munster. Notable ranges include MacGillycuddy's Reeks, the Cahas, the Galtys, the Knockmealdowns and the Comeraghs. The Provincial High Point of Munster is Carrauntoohil in Kerry (chapter 1).

MacGillycuddy's Reeks viewed from north Kerry

1. COUNTY
KERRY

Kerry is a coastal county in the southwest of Ireland. With an area of 4,748km² it is the fifth largest county in Ireland and the second largest in Munster. It shares land boundaries with two other counties: Limerick and Cork.

Notable Geographical Facts about Kerry

Kerry is number 1 on the Irish county height rankings. It is the most westerly county in Ireland.

Ireland's twelve highest peaks are in Kerry – eleven in MacGillycuddy's Reeks. All but two of Ireland's peaks above 3,000 feet are in Kerry – the other two are Lugnaquillia Mountain in Wicklow (chapter 21) and Galtymore Mountain on the Limerick/Tipperary boundary (chapters 2 and 3).

Cummeenoughter Lake in Kerry is the highest natural lake in Ireland, 707m above sea level, between Carrauntoohil and Beenkeragh in MacGillycuddy's Reeks.

County Kerry

CARRAUNTOOHIL

The metal cross at the 1,039m summit of Carrauntoohil marks the CHP of Kerry at **V:804:844**. OSi maps indicate the presence of a triangulation station at the summit, but there is currently no trig pillar on Carrauntoohil. A small patch of concrete, metal and timber a short distance west of the summit cross matches the dimensions of a trig pillar – archive photos show that a pillar was indeed present here. This summit in MacGillycuddy's Reeks is classed as a Hewitt, a Marilyn and a Vandeleur-Lynam. It has the added distinctions of being the Provincial High Point of Munster, the National High Point of the Republic of Ireland and the highest point in Ireland as a whole. It is also the most westerly CHP in Munster. Carrauntoohil is often incorrectly referred to as a Munro – a classification type reserved for certain Scottish summits higher than 3,000 feet (914.4m) above sea level.

Carrauntoohil summit is 12.2km south-southeast of Killorglin, 17.4km west-southwest of Killarney and 17.1km northwest of Kenmare. Any of these locations would make a suitable base for exploring Carrauntoohil, MacGillycuddy's Reeks and the surrounding area.

Route Summary:

Providing the safest approach to Carrauntoohil summit, this out-and-back route follows a clear track through the popular Hag's Glen. Two steep sections – the Zig-zags and the final approach to the summit – require a good level of fitness, but are generally quite easy to follow. The top and bottom of the Zig-zags, however, are not obvious and can be difficult to locate. As a result, many people continue to use the Devil's Ladder gully despite warnings of its potential dangers.

Time: 4½ to 7 hours **Distance:** 14.1km
Ascent: 1,000m **Grading:** Challenging
Access Restrictions: None
Maps: OSi Sheet 78; OSi *MacGillycuddy's Reeks*;
Harvey Superwalker *MacGillycuddy's Reeks*

Start/Finish: Cronin's Yard at **V:836:874** where there is a car park, a café, toilets and shower facilities. This is 4.4km northeast of the CHP. Parking costs €2. In-car satnav coordinates for Cronin's Yard are: (a) **N52°01'35.67"**, **W9°41'45.22"** or (b) **N52.026576°, W9.695894°**.

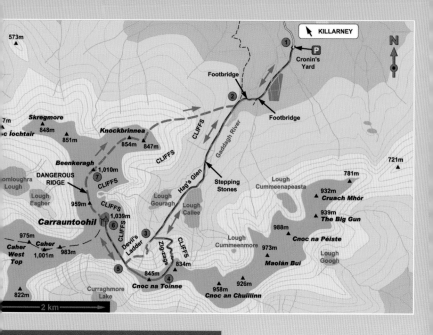

Route Description

(1) Cronin's Yard (V:83648:87363:138)

Locate the memorials on a wall at the southern end of Cronin's Yard. Pass through the gate to their right, and follow the track in a southwesterly direction. Pass through a second gate and cross a concrete bridge. Continue along the track and cross the first of two new metal footbridges. After a short distance, go right at a fork and descend to the second metal footbridge. Cross this, and follow track uphill to a Y-junction.

(2) Y-junction in track (V:82714:86445:233)

Take the track to the left and continue up Hag's Glen along the right-hand side of the Gaddagh River. Cross a tributary at some stepping stones. Pass between Lough Callee and Lough Gouragh. Continue towards the lowest col straight ahead where the eroded Devil's Ladder gully forms an obvious ascent route. About 200m before the bottom of the Devil's Ladder, look for a boulder beside the path with a small stone cairn built upon it. This cairn marks the turn-off for the Bóthar na Gíge zig-zags (generally referred to as the Zig-zags), but it can easily be missed. If you arrive at the bottom of the Devil's Ladder, turn around to face back the way you have just come. Look for a grassy ramp to the right-hand side of the path rising in an easterly direction and away from Carrauntoohil. This ramp leads towards the Zig-zags.

Carrauntoohil viewed from Hag's Glen

(3) Cairn marking start of Zig-zags (V: 81150:84071:453)

Follow the ramp upwards. This is not an obvious worn path and may be muddy at the start. Continue uphill in an easterly direction and the Zig-zags will reveal themselves. When they do, follow the steep zig-zag path to reach a broad ridge near Cnoc na Toinne summit.

(4) Top of Zig-zags (V:81371,83448:825)

Turn right along the broad ridge and over Cnoc na Toinne summit. Descend west-northwest along the centre line of a peaty ridge to arrive at the top of the Devil's Ladder.

(5) Top of Devil's Ladder (V:80682:83668:731)

Continue northwest across the col, then along an obvious path which zig-zags steeply to the summit. Arrive at the metal cross – the CHP of Kerry.

(6) Carrauntoohil summit (V:80361:84425:1039)

Retrace your steps to (1). Be sure to take a southerly departure from Carrauntoohil summit in order to pick up the path back to (5) – if you find yourself on a clear path heading southwest, you have strayed onto the Caher ridge. Also, when ascending Cnoc na Toinne from (5), keep a central line along the stepped peaty ridge – it falls away on both sides. Care also needs to be taken on the steep descent of the Zig-zags.

Bottom of the Zig-zags

Special Note:

Do not attempt to descend from Carrauntoohil summit towards the general direction of north, northeast, east or southeast. There are no safe routes on these sides of the summit. Extra care needs to be taken on the summit area during strong winds.

OPTION A: Alternative ascent from (3) to (5) via the Devil's Ladder

The Devil's Ladder provides the shortest and most direct route from (3) to (5) (or vice versa) eliminating the need to pass (4). If you choose this route, extra care needs to be taken (see special note below).

Option A saves 1.1km of horizontal distance and up to 30 minutes in each direction. It also reduces the amount of vertical ascent in each direction by 110m.

Special Note:

While the Devil's Ladder provides the shortest and most direct approach to Carrauntoohil summit, its use is currently not being recommended. Due to unstable terrain and continued erosion, there is a serious risk of rock falls.

OPTION B: Alternative descent route from (6) to (2) via Beenkeragh

From the summit at (6), head west initially for a short distance to arrive at a path junction. Head right and northwest along a path. Proceed carefully down to the start of the Beenkeragh ridge, passing the tops of three gullies (namely Curved, Central and O'Shea's) which all descend to the right. Cross the Beenkeragh ridge. Utmost care is needed here! The requirement to use your hands is likely. Follow a narrow worn path northwards along the ridge. This faint path occasionally switches sides of the high line. Keep north for a short distance past the end of the ridge before heading northeast across rocks to approach Ireland's second highest summit: Beenkeragh.

(7) Beenkeragh summit (V:80128:85247:1010)

Descend northeast from the summit, then cross a wide col to Knockbrinnea's west summit at **V:80775:85821:854**. Follow the high line to the east summit at **V:81019:85742:847**. Descend north-northeast, curving right towards northwest to avoid scree and cliffs on the right. Adjust course if necessary on the lower slopes to arrive at the path junction at (2) **(V:82714:86445:233)**. Take the path descending northeast towards the river, and cross the two new footbridges on the return to Cronin's Yard.

Special Note:

The notorious Beenkeragh Ridge is not for the faint-hearted. It is a particularly hazardous section and demands a good head for heights, balance and sure footing. It is not a recommended route option in windy and/or icy conditions. By including the alternative descent route, the overall grading for this walk increases to 'demanding'.

Metal cross marking County High Point of Kerry at Carrauntoohil summit

2. COUNTY
LIMERICK

Limerick is a coastal county in the southwest of Ireland. With an area of 2,687km², it is the tenth largest county in Ireland and the fifth largest in Munster. It shares land boundaries with four other counties: Clare, Tipperary, Cork and Kerry.

Notable Geographical Facts about Limerick

Limerick is number 3 on the Irish county height rankings.

With a length of approximately 53km, Limerick has the sixteenth longest county coastline in Ireland. This is also the shortest among the coastal counties of Munster.

Galtymore Mountain

Points on this summit represent the CHPs of Limerick and neighbouring Tipperary. Refer to Chapter 3 – County Tipperary – for information about Galtymore Mountain and its walking route description.

It is worth noting that the highest unshared summit lying entirely within Limerick is that of Lyracappul at **R:846:232**. Its 825m summit is located in the Galty range, 3.4km west of the CHP.

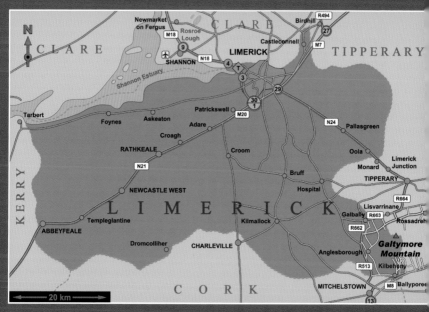

County Limerick

3. COUNTY
TIPPERARY

Tipperary is a landlocked county in the south of Ireland. With an area of 4,305km², it is the sixth largest county in Ireland and the third largest in Munster. It shares boundaries with eight other counties: Waterford, Cork, Limerick, Clare, Galway, Offaly, Laois and Kilkenny.

Notable Geographical Facts about Tipperary

Tipperary is number 4 on the Irish county height rankings.
Tipperary has a county height of 917m – the greatest among the landlocked counties in Ireland. Tipperary is also the largest landlocked county in Ireland. The highest unshared summit lying entirely within Tipperary is that of Greenane at **R:925:239**. Its 802m summit is located 4.6km east of the CHP.

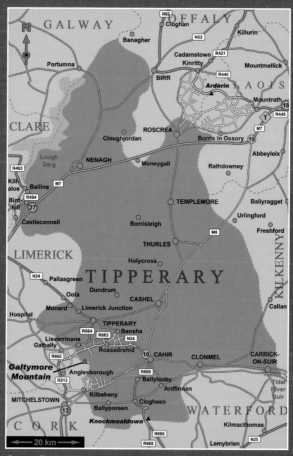

County Tipperary

GALTYMORE MOUNTAIN

The stone cairn at the 919m summit of Galtymore Mountain marks the CHP of Limerick at **R:87848:23793:919**. The CHP of Tipperary is the top of the nearby broken trig pillar at **R:87851:23795:919**, through which the county boundary passes. These two CHPs are separated horizontally by less than 10m – the shortest distance between two unshared CHPs in Ireland. There is also a white cross on the summit area and a second cairn further west. This summit in the Galty Mountains is classed as a Hewitt, a Marilyn and a Vandeleur-Lynam. Galtymore Mountain is often incorrectly referred to as being a Munro – a classification type reserved only for certain Scottish summits higher than 3,000 feet (914.4m) above sea level.

Galtymore Mountain summit is 11.9km south of Tipperary, 12.9km north-northeast of Mitchelstown and 17.2km west of Cahir. Any of these locations would make a suitable base for exploring Galtymore Mountain, the Galty Mountains and the surrounding area.

Route Summary

This out-and-back route initially follows a quiet road before a short section across grazing land leads onto the steep mountainsides. Good navigation skills are required as there are cliffs close to the route. An ascent variation and an alternative descent via Slievecushnabinnia have also been described.

Time: 3½ to 5¾ hours **Distance:** 10.9km
Ascent: 870m **Grading:** Challenging
Access Restrictions: None identified **Map:** OSi Sheet 74.

Start/Finish: R:874:278 near the start of a cul-de-sac road where there is an official car park. This is 4km north of the CHPs. The cul-de-sac road starts from an unsigned junction at **R:875:281**. In-car satnav coordinates for the start are: (a) **N52°24'15.23", W8°11'04.33"** or (b) **N52.404231°, W8.184536°**.

Route Description

(1) Car park near Clydagh Bridge (R:87434:27776:126)

From the car park entrance, turn right along the tarmac towards the south. Follow this all the way to its end where there are two gated entrances. Pass through the gate on the right to follow a track onto grazing land.

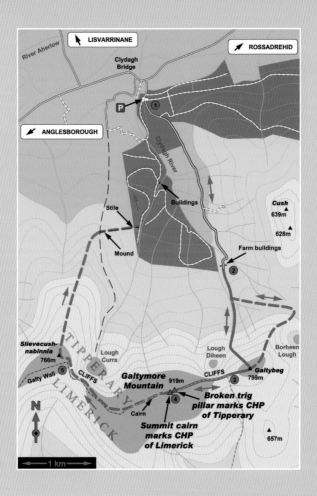

(2) End of track onto farmland (R:88554:25463:305)

Continue south and parallel to a fence on the left. Continue straight and in a general southerly direction beyond the corner of the fence. Aim towards the low point between Galtybeg and Galtymore Mountain. Cross any streams encountered on this short ascent until Lough Diheen comes into view ahead. Veer left towards the southeast for a steep ascent to Galtybeg summit at **R:88989:24098:799**. Turn right east-southeast and descend to the peaty col.

Galtymore Mountain viewed from the northern slopes of Galtybeg

(3) Col between Galtybeg and Galtymore Mountain (R:88595:23998:722)

Follow a clear path ascending west-southwest. Do not stray too far to the right as there are cliffs on that side. Negotiate your way over and between peat banks where necessary. Ground becomes rockier on the higher ground. Arrive at CHPs of Tipperary and Limerick on Galtymore Mountain summit.

(4) Galtymore Mountain summit (R:87848:23793:919)

Retrace your steps to (1).

Special Note:

Extra care needs to be taken on Galtymore Mountain and its eastern and western cols during strong south-to-north crosswinds.

OPTION A: (2) to (3) via col between Cush and Galtybeg

Proceed south from (2). Follow the fence on the left to where it turns. Turn left at this point towards the east and ascend to the col between Cush and Galtybeg. Turn right and continue up and over Galtybeg summit to arrive at (3).

Option A adds 0.6km to the horizontal distance and 10–30 minutes in each direction. It has no effect on the amount of vertical ascent.

Cairn marking the County High Point of Limerick and trig pillar marking that of Tipperary at Galtymore Mountain summit.

OPTION B: Alternative descent from (4) to (1) via Slievecushnabinnia

From (4), continue west-southwest across the summit area and Dawson's Table. Pass a white cross and memorials on the right and a stone cairn marking the start of the descent. Drop down to the peaty col to pick up the Galty Wall. Follow the wall as it curves right towards the northwest to arrive at a right-angled corner to the left.

(5) Corner of Galty Wall on Slievecushnabinnia (R:86346:24197:758)

Turn left along the wall for a short distance, veering right from it slightly to arrive at a strange stone configuration comprised of three small cairns. From here, head north-northeast on a grid bearing of 12° to follow the Knocknanuss spur. Descend to meet the Lough Curra track.

(6) Track to Lough Curra (R:86873:25857:355)

Cross the track and head east, passing over an obvious mound. Enter the forest by crossing the stile and continue to where the path meets a forest track. Turn left along the track. Avoid a side track to the left. Arrive at a junction with some buildings and a tower ahead. Turn left here and follow track back to start point.

Option B adds 1.5km of horizontal distance and up to 30 minutes to the descent. It also decreases the vertical ascent by 40m.

4. COUNTY
WATERFORD

Waterford is a coastal county in the south of Ireland. With an area of 1,838km², it is the twenty-second largest county in Ireland and the smallest in Munster. It shares land boundaries with three other counties: Cork, Tipperary and Kilkenny.

Notable Geographical Facts about Waterford

Waterford is number 9 on the Irish county height rankings.

It is the most easterly county in Munster. The easternmost point in Munster is Creadan Head at **S:718:035**, which is 4.2km northeast of the village of Dunmore East.

The highest unshared summit lying entirely within Waterford is that of Fauscoum at **S:317:105.** Its 792m summit is located in the Comeragh Mountains 26km to the east of the CHP.

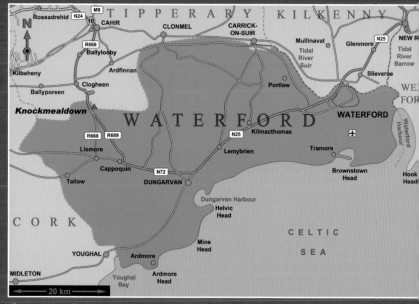

County Waterford

KNOCKMEALDOWN

The trig pillar at the 794m summit of Knockmealdown marks the CHP of Waterford at **S:058:084** on the county boundary with Tipperary. This summit in the Knockmealdown Mountains is classed as a Hewitt, a Marilyn and a Vandeleur-Lynam. It has the added distinction of being the most easterly CHP in Munster.

Knockmealdown summit is 10.3km north of Lismore, 16.5km south of Cahir and 24.7km east of Mitchelstown. Any of these locations would make a suitable base for exploring Knockmealdown, the Knockmealdown Mountains and the surrounding area.

Knockmealdown viewed from the west

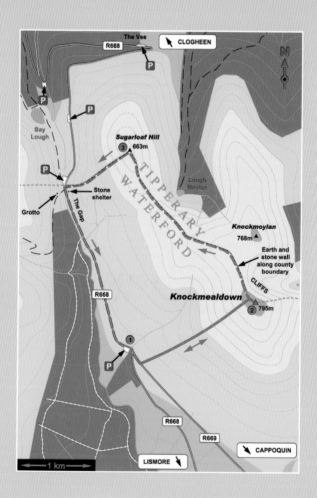

Route Summary

This out-and-back route is the shortest approach to Knockmealdown. It is an ascent of moderate steepness through heather all the way to the summit. An optional descent via Sugarloaf Hill is also given.

Time: 1¾ to 2½ hours   **Distance:** 4.3km
Ascent: 525m   **Grading:** Moderate
Access Restrictions: None   **Map:** OSi Sheet 74.

Start/Finish: at **S:040:078** at a car park beside the R668. This is 1.9km west-southwest of the CHP. In-car satnav coordinates for the start/finish are: (a) **N52°13'20.45", W7°56'33.32"** or (b) **N52.222347°, W7.942589°**.

Route Description
(1) Car park on R688 (S:03985:07786:270)
Carefully cross the road from the car park and turn right along the R668 for a short distance to arrive at a junction. Take the R669 on the left. At any convenient opportunity, turn left off the road and head northeast, aiming slightly left of Knockmealdown summit. Follow any of the faint paths through the heather that allow you to keep moving up towards the northeast. Keep left of some rocky patches near the top. Arrive on the high line of the ridge where a steep drop into neighbouring Tipperary awaits. Turn right to the southeast, and ascend to the trig pillar – the CHP of Waterford.

Trig pillar marking the County High Point of Waterford at Knockmealdown summit

(2) Knockmealdown summit (S:05801:08410:794)

Retrace your steps to (1).

Special Note:

Extra care needs to be taken on the summit area of Knockmealdown during strong southwest-to-northeast crosswinds.

OPTION A: Alternative descent from (2) to (1)
via Sugarloaf Hill

From (2), descend northwest initially and follow the ridge as it curves right towards the north-northwest. The remains of an earth and stone wall form the Waterford/Tipperary boundary along this ridge. Follow the boundary all the way to Sugarloaf Hill summit.

(3) Sugarloaf Hill summit (S:03972:10478:663)

Descend from the summit along the county boundary wall towards the west-southwest to arrive at the R668 close to a car park. This walk can easily be adapted to start and finish from here. Turn left to follow the road south-southeast. An off-road path to the left-hand side can also be used instead of the road in places. Stay close to the road and follow its general line to the start point.

Option A adds 4.3km of horizontal distance and up to 2 hours to the descent. It also increases the vertical ascent by 140m.

Sugarloaf Hill with the Galty Mountains beyond

5. COUNTY
CORK

Cork is a coastal county in the southwest corner of Ireland. With an area of 7,460km², it is the largest county in Ireland. It shares land boundaries with four other counties: Limerick, Tipperary, Waterford and Kerry.

Notable Geographical Facts about Cork

Cork is number 13 on the Irish county height rankings.

It is the most southerly county in Ireland.

With a length of approximately 540km, Cork's county coastline is the second longest in Ireland and the longest in Munster.

The highest unshared summit lying entirely within Cork is that of Hungry Hill at **V:761:497**. Its 685m summit is located in the Caha Mountains 27.3km to the west-southwest of the CHP.

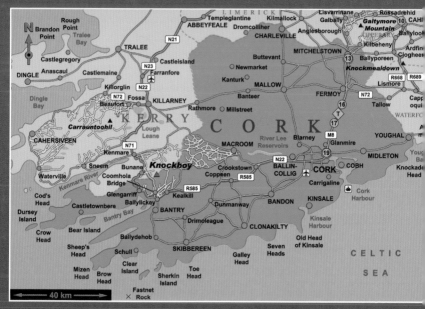

County Cork

KNOCKBOY

The trig pillar at the 706m summit of Knockboy marks the CHP of Cork at **W:005:621** on the county boundary with Kerry. This summit in the Shehy Mountains is classed as a Hewitt, a Marilyn and a Vandeleur-Lynam. It has the added distinction of being the most southerly CHP in Ireland.

Knockboy summit is 9.5km northeast of Glengarriff , 13.1km southeast of Kenmare and 13.4km north of Bantry. Any of these locations would make a suitable base for exploring Knockboy, the Shehy Mountains and the surrounding area.

Route Summary

This out-and-back route follows the Cork/Kerry boundary from the mountain pass at Priest's Leap. There are some moderately steep sections, boggy areas and rock outcrops along its course. The route described also involves six fence crossings (i.e. three in each direction), although this number can be reduced by keeping to the Kerry side of the county boundary.

Time: 1¾ to 2½ hours **Distance:** 5.2km
Ascent: 230m **Grading:** Moderate
Access Restrictions: None identified, although no stiles at fences
Map: OSi Sheet 85.

Start/Finish: Priest's Leap at **V:985:611**, where there is roadside parking for up to four cars. This is 2.2km west-southwest of the CHP. In-car satnav coordinates for Priest's Leap are: (a) **N51°47'36.45", W9°28'16.77"** or (b) **N51.793458°, W9.471325°**.

Lough Reagh and Lough Boy with Knockboy beyond

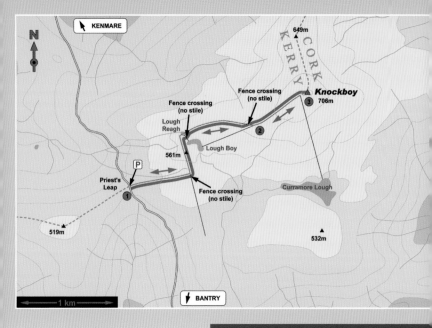

Route Description

(1) Car park at Priest's Leap (V:98537:61095:472)

From the small car parking area, head east-northeast across the road. Pass to the right of the corner in the fence for direct access onto mountain land. Keep the fence to your left and proceed uphill to the east-northeast until your path is blocked by another fence. Cross this fence here at a sturdy post. Turn left, keeping the fence to your left as you continue north-northwest and over a minor 561m summit to arrive at a right-angled bend to the right. Continue along the fence to the east-northeast. Pass between Lough Reagh and Lough Boy, crossing a low fence that connects them. Rejoin the main fence line and follow it eastwards. Cross to the other side of this fence at a suitable point and keep it on your right until you arrive at another fence junction.

(2) Fence junction (V:99813:61681:611)

Veer left, keeping to the main fence and follow uphill east-northeast to arrive at a right-angled bend to the right. Trig pillar should now be in sight. Continue straight past this right-angled bend to arrive at the trig pillar – the CHP of Cork.

(3) Knockboy summit (W:00481:62060:706)

Retrace your steps to (1).

Follow this fence to Knockboy summit

OPTION A: Alternative route from (1) to (3)

It is possible to reduce the number of fence crossings along this route by keeping to the Kerry side of the county boundary. This can be achieved by crossing the fence at Priest's Leap and following the county boundary fence uphill towards east-northeast. Keeping the fence to your right at all times on the ascent will bring you to the summit of Knockboy.

Trig pillar marking the County High Point of Cork at Knockboy summit

6. COUNTY
CLARE

Clare is a coastal county in the southwest of Ireland. With an area of 3,191km², it is the eighth largest county in Ireland and the fourth largest in Munster. It shares land boundaries with three other counties Tipperary, Limerick and Galway.

Notable Geographical Facts about Clare

Clare is number 23 on the Irish county height rankings.

It is the most northerly county in Munster. The northernmost point in Munster is at **M:287:137** on Aughinish, an island linked to neighbouring Galway by a causeway, 8km northeast of Ballyvaughan. The island was previously linked to mainland Clare until 1755 when that connection was removed as the result of a tsunami triggered by an earthquake in Portugal.

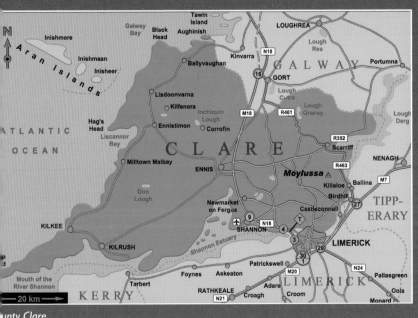

County Clare

MOYLUSSA

The unfurnished 532m summit of Moylussa is a CHP of Clare at **R:648:759**. While this point is regarded by some to be the only CHP of Clare, Moylussa also has a second 532m summit located 450m to the southeast at **R:652:756** – verifying which of these is the true summit would require precise survey measurements. For the purposes of this book, these twin summits jointly share the honour of being the CHPs of Clare. It is, therefore, recommended that both locations be visited if undertaking a CHP walk. Moylussa lies in the Slieve Bearnagh Mountains. It is classed as a Marilyn, and is the most northerly CHP in Munster.

Moylussa viewed from the east

Moylussa's twin summits are 6.1km west-northwest of Killaloe–Ballina and 8.9km south of Scarriff. Any of these locations would make a suitable base for exploring Moylussa, the Slieve Bearnagh Mountains and the surrounding area.

Route Summary
This out-and-back route is predominantly on well-kept forest tracks and paths, including waymarked sections of the East Clare Way and Coillte's waymarked Crag Wood Walk. One section of the route also passes through a notoriously

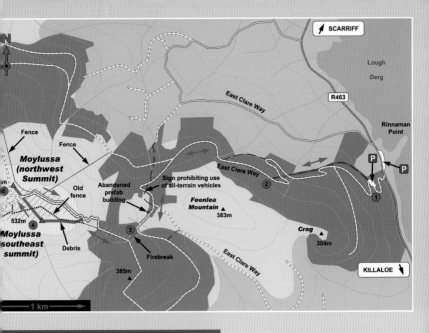

boggy firebreak. From this, a steep, stony track leads to near the summit area. A short loop passes over the twin summits. This route is not recommended after prolonged wet weather.

Time: 3 to 5 hours **Distance:** 10.6km
Ascent: 480m **Grading:** Moderate
Access Restrictions: None identified, although no stiles at fences
Map: OSi Sheet 58.

Start/Finish: Ballycuggaran Forest car park at **R:686:760**. This is 3.6km east of the CHPs. Ballycuggaran Forest is accessed via its main entrance at **R:688:760** along the R463 between Killaloe and Scarriff. In-car satnav coordinates for the entrance to Ballycuggaran Forest are: (a) **N52°50'06.25", W8°27'51.90"** or (b) **N52.835069°, W8.464417°**.

Route Description
(1) Car park at Ballycuggaran Forest (R:68632:75975:080)
Pass the right of the two metal barriers at the top end of the car park. Proceed uphill along the path heading northwest. Emerge onto the zig-zagging forest track and turn right along it for a short distance to where it bends sharply to the left. Leave the track at this point and continue straight along the waymarked path uphill. Keep straight along the path (as waymarked) on the next two occasions where it crosses the same zig-zagging track. Arrive at a T-junction with the track.

Boggy forest track leading towards Moylussa

(2) Join forest track where path ends (R:67587:76004:225)

Turn right and proceed along the forest track (as waymarked). Avoid all side paths to arrive at a forked junction. Take the left track forking uphill and follow it, avoiding all side paths. Pass a sign on the right prohibiting the use of all-terrain vehicles. Stay on the main track. At the next junction, the East Clare Way is waymarked to the left. Ignore this turn-off, and keep straight. An abandoned prefab building comes into view among the trees to the right soon after. Pass this and a large clearing immediately on your right. After a short distance, the forest track bends left. Arrive at the start of a firebreak on this bend.

(3) Start of path at firebreak (R:66137:75484:348)

Turn right off the forest track and follow the right-hand side of the firebreak to the southwest. Beware of a deep drainage ditch running down the middle of the firebreak – keep to the right of it. The ground here can be very boggy, so tread carefully. Arrive at a three-way junction in the firebreak. Take the wide, peaty one on the right and follow it west-northwest. Again, this is a boggy section. A drier line can be found running along the left-hand side, although it is partly overgrown in places. Arrive at the end of the firebreak where a steep, stony track begins. Follow this as it zig-zags up the hillside to where it meets a fence. Cross this fence. From here, proceed west along a faint path through heather. Maintain this course past some scattered wreckage to arrive at a landmark composed of sticks and pieces of carved timber bearing the names 'Brian Boru', 'Cusack', 'Foley' and 'Lohan'. One of Clare's CHPs – the southeast summit of Moylussa – is located at an unmarked location just 3m beyond this landmark to its west-northwest.

(4) Moylussa's southeast summit (R:65115:75573:532)

On a grid bearing of 321° proceed towards Moylussa's northwest summit, which is 450m away. The flat, featureless area between the summits can be quite boggy in places. Pass a line of posts marking an old fence line and cross a brown, peaty track to arrive at Clare's other CHP – the unmarked northwest summit of Moylussa.

(5) Moylussa's northwest summit (R:64835:75928:532)

Head southeast off this summit for a short distance to pick up the brown, peaty track you crossed earlier. Turn left to follow it east-northeast. A fence comes in from the left and runs along the left-hand side of the track which turns right to the east-southeast. Follow the track through the fence. The peaty track becomes the steep, stony track you ascended earlier. Descend along this and retrace your steps to (1).

Option A: Zig-zagging forest track between (1) and (2)

At (1), pass the left of the two metal barriers at the top end of the car park. From here, follow the zig-zagging forest track to (2).

Option A adds 1.3km to the horizontal distance and up to 30 minutes in each direction. It has no affect on the amount of vertical ascent, but reduces the incline between (1) and (2).

Moylussa southeast summit (foreground left) and Moylussa northwest summit (background) – the twin County High Points of Clare

CONNACHT

Covering the western quarter of Ireland, the province of Connacht comprises the five counties of Mayo, Galway, Sligo, Leitrim and Roscommon. With an area of 17,711km^2, Connacht is the smallest of Ireland's four provinces. Notable mountain ranges include the Mweelrea Mountains, the Twelve Bens (or Twelve Pins), the Maumturks, the Nephins and the Dartrys. The Provincial High Point of Connacht is Mweelrea in Mayo (chapter 7).

*Doo Lough near Mweelrea,
County Mayo*

7. COUNTY
MAYO

Mayo is a coastal county in the west of Ireland. With an area of 5,587km², it is the third largest county in Ireland and the second largest in Connacht. It shares land boundaries with three other counties: Sligo, Roscommon and Galway.

Notable Geographical Facts about Mayo
Mayo is number 6 on the Irish county height rankings.
By including its islands, Mayo is the most westerly county in Connacht.
The highest sea cliffs in Ireland and the third highest in Europe can be found in Mayo. These form the northern side of Croaghaun on Achill Island. From the 688m summit, there is an almost sheer drop into the Atlantic Ocean.

County Mayo

MWEELREA

The stone cairn at the 814m summit of Mweelrea marks the CHP of Mayo at **L:790:668**. This summit in the Mweelrea Mountains is classed as a Hewitt, a Marilyn and a Vandeleur-Lynam, and it is the Provincial High Point of Connacht. It is also the most coastal CHP in Ireland – just 1.6km from Killary Harbour.

Mweelrea summit lies 14.1km south of Louisburgh, 10.1km west-northwest of Leenaun and 27.5km southwest of Westport. Any of these locations would make a suitable base for exploring Mweelrea, the Mweelrea Mountains and the surrounding area.

Route Summary

This out-and-back route provides the safest and most direct approach to Mweelrea summit. A short track at the start leads to open mountain land which can be boggy in places. The final approach to the summit is quite rocky and crosses small boulder fields. Sound navigation skills are required on this route, especially in poor visibility.

Mweelrea viewed from the northwest

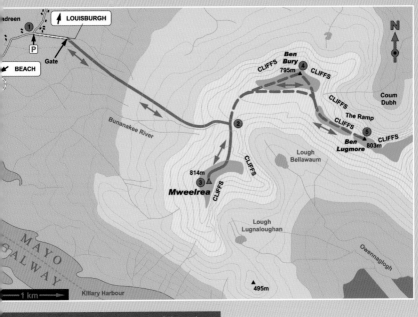

Mweelrea

Time: 3 to 5 hours ***Distance:*** 8.6km
Ascent: 780m Grading: Moderate
Access Restrictions: None identified ***Map:*** OSi Sheet 37.

Start/Finish: the entrance to a rough farm track marked by a cul-de-sac sign
at **L:764:688**, 3.3km northwest of the CHP. It is possible for up to three cars
to park here provided that you do not block the track for others. A car park
can also be found at the public beach about 1km further along the road. In-
car satnav coordinates for the farm track entrance are: (a) **N53°39'17.04",
W9°52'10.05"** or (b) **N53.654733°, W9.869458°**.

Route Description
(1) Entrance to farm track (L:76448:68822:039)
Follow the stony farm track eastwards to a gate at **L:76868:68801:088**. Pass
through the gate to enter open mountain land. Proceed east-southeast, crossing
streams and boggy ground. If it is visible, aim for the col between Ben Bury on
the left and Mweelrea on the right. If visibility is poor, follow a grid bearing of
approximately 120°. On approach to the col, a stream has cut an obvious channel.
Follow this eastwards to the col.

The approach to Mweelrea from (2)

(2) Col between Ben Bury and Mweelrea (L:79298:67603:648)

Turn right and continue southwards to begin the final approach to Mweelrea summit. From here the terrain becomes boulder-strewn in places. Avoid a spur branching eastwards to the left. Continue the ascent by veering slightly right in a southwesterly direction before a final southward approach. Arrive at the summit cairn – the CHP of Mayo.

(3) Mweelrea summit (L:78977:66813:814)

Retrace your steps back to the start point. From the summit take an initial northward descent, curving right to the northeast. Again, avoid the spur branching eastwards to the right. Continue northwards to the col at (2). Descend westwards from the col to follow the obvious stream channel before veering west-northwest across boggy ground on a grid bearing of approximately 300° to arrive at the gate **(L:76868:68801:088)**. Follow the stony farm track back to the start.

OPTION A: Out-and back extension to Ben Lugmore from (2)

Having returned to (2) on the descent, continue straight along the ridge in a northerly direction. Follow the high line of this broad ridge as it curves right. Do not stray too far left as there are cliffs to that side. Arrive at the cairn marking Ben Bury summit.

Mayo: Mweelrea

(4) Ben Bury summit (L:80255:68281:795)

Head southeast from the summit. Meet cliffs on the left. Follow the cliff top south along the rim of Coum Dubh and descend to a col where a path can be seen descending into the corrie along the Ramp. Ignore this path, and continue south-southeast and up along the ridge. Carefully follow a distinct path to arrive at the highest point on the ridge – Ben Lugmore summit.

(5) Ben Lugmore summit (L:81171:67378:803)

Retrace steps back to the col at (2). Bypass Ben Bury summit on the return by keeping close to the 750m contour along its southern side. Beware of the cliffs on the right when rejoining the broad ridge. Descend along the high line of the ridge to (2). Descend westwards from (2), and return to the start point as per the main route described earlier.

Option A adds 5.4km of horizontal distance and up to 3 hours to the route. It also increases the vertical ascent by 350m.

Special Note:

The ridge between (4) and (5) is a hazardous section and requires a good head for heights, balance and sure footing. It is not a recommended route option in windy or icy conditions. By including the optional ridge section, the overall grading for this walk increases to 'demanding'.

Cairn marking the County High Point of Mayo at Mweelrea summit

8. COUNTY
GALWAY

Galway is a coastal county in the west of Ireland. With an area of 6,150km², it is the second largest county in Ireland and the largest in Connacht. It shares land boundaries with five other counties: Mayo, Roscommon, Offaly, Tipperary and Clare.

Notable Geographical Facts about Galway

Galway is number 12 on the Irish county height rankings.

It is the most westerly mainland county in Connacht. Galway is also the most southerly county in Connacht.

The geographical centre of the Republic of Ireland **(M:754:418)** is in Galway, 3.9km northwest of the village of Ahascragh.

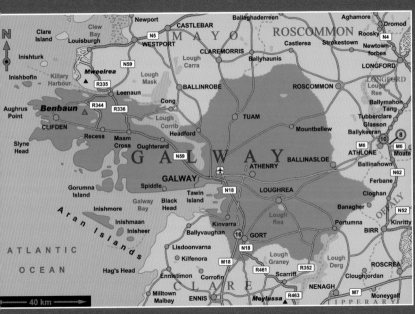

unty Galway

BENBAUN

The broken trig pillar at the 729m summit of Benbaun marks the CHP of Galway at **L:786:539**. This summit in the Twelve Bens is classed as a Hewitt, a Marilyn and a Vandeleur-Lynam. It is the most westerly CHP in Ireland – beating Mweelrea in Mayo by just 400m – and the most southerly in Connacht. It should not be confused with the nearby 477m summit of the same name at **L:765:568**, which is 3.6km to the northwest.

Benbaun summit is 8.5km east-southeast of Letterfrack, 12.3km southwest of Leenaun and 13km east-northeast of Clifden. Any of these locations would make a suitable base for exploring Benbaun, the Twelve Bens and the surrounding area.

Route Summary

This out-and-back route from Glencorbet initially follows a stony track before a steep ascent up the valley side onto rocky terrain. Steep, grassy sections may be slippery, and the final approach to the summit is a zig-zagging path through loose rock and scree.

Time: 3 to 5 hours *Distance:* 8.8km
Ascent: 710m *Grading:* Challenging
Access Restrictions: None
Maps: OSi Sheet 37; Harvey Superwalker *Connemara*.

Start/Finish: at **L:796:573** where a stony farm track meets a tarmac laneway, 3.6km north-northeast of the CHP. It is possible to park beside the tarmac laneway between the start/finish and the bridge at **L:800:574**. In-car satnav coordinates for the start/finish are: (a) **N53°33'08.59", W9°49'01.91"** or (b) **N53.552386°, W9.817197°**.

Route Description
(1) Start point in Glencorbet (L:79622:57343:041)
Take the stony track on the left-hand side of the lane. Proceed south and follow uphill. The track drops to meet the Kylemore River, and follows its northern bank to arrive at a ford. Beware of slippery rocks when crossing here. Continue along the track on the southern bank. Ignore a side track off to the left. Stay on the track until it begins to curve left and away from the river. Go off the track here by keeping straight to follow the river west-southwest. Keep between the river on the right and the fence on the left. Follow a worn path to arrive at a left-hand corner in the fence.

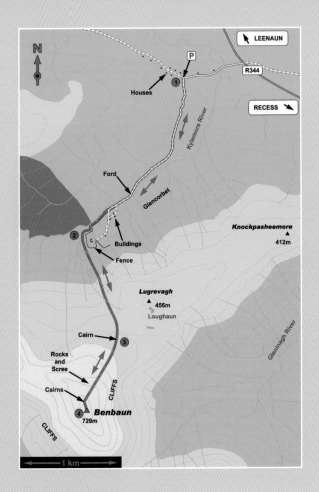

(2) Corner of fence beside river (L:78555:55755:120)

Enter open mountain land. Turn left. Follow the fence south initially until it turns left and eastwards. Depart from the fence, keeping south, then south-southeast uphill. Aim slightly right of the col between Benbaun and Lugrevagh. There is no clear path to follow here. Several streams will have to be crossed from left to right. Pick your own route on this steep uphill section, keeping towards the south-southeast. The ground becomes rockier as you approach the broad ridge. Find the stone cairn indicating the route to the summit.

Benbaun viewed from Glencorbet

(3) Cairn marking route to Benbaun (L:78886:54620:488)

The path is not an obvious one, but you will find it by heading southwest towards Benbaun summit. The ground becomes steeper near the summit where the path passes through rocks and scree. Some minor scrambling may be required on the final steep section. Arrive on the summit ridge close to a stone cairn – this will be your marker when starting the descent. Turn left and continue south-southeast past a second cairn to arrive at the broken trig pillar – the CHP of Galway.

(4) Benbaun summit (L:78556:53904:729)

Retrace your steps to (I).

Approaching the col between Benbaun and Lugrevagh

*Broken trig pillar marking the County High
Point of Galway at Benbaun summit*

9. COUNTY
SLIGO

Sligo is a coastal county in the northwest of Ireland. With an area of 1,837km², it is the twenty-third largest county in Ireland and the fourth largest in Connacht. It shares land boundaries with three other counties: Leitrim, Roscommon and Mayo.

Notable Geographical Facts about Sligo

Sligo is number 18 on the Irish county height rankings.

At high tide, Sligo becomes the most northerly county in Connacht as a whole. This is on the north side of Hugh's Island at **G:705:586** just off Mullaghmore Head. (At low tide, however, Leitrim becomes the most northerly county in Connacht at approximately **G:787:587** just north of the village of Tullaghan.)

...unty Sligo

TRUSKMORE

Truskmore viewed from Gleniff

The trig pillar at the 647m summit of Truskmore marks the CHP of Sligo at **G:759:473**. The summit area is dominated by a large RTÉ NL transmitter site. This summit in the Dartry Mountains is classed as a Hewitt, a Marilyn and a Vandeleur-Lynam, and is the most northerly CHP in Connacht.

Truskmore summit is 13.1km south-southwest of Bundoran, 13.3km north-northeast of Sligo and 14.8km west-northwest of Manorhamilton. Any of these locations would make a suitable base for exploring Truskmore, the Dartry Mountains and the surrounding area.

The Truskmore route described here includes an optional extension to Truskmore Southeast Slope.

Route Summary

A straightforward out-and-back walk along the RTÉ NL access road leading to the large telecommunications mast at Truskmore summit. The route has a gentle incline – moderate in places – and the CHP is clearly marked by a trig pillar on a stone cairn located to the northwest of the compound. It is best to avoid this summit during wintry conditions, due to the risk of ice falling from the mast and its guy wires, and when maintenance work is being carried out.

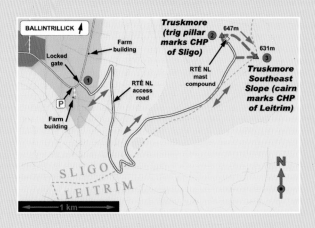

Time: 2½ to 4 hours ***Distance:*** 8.4km
Ascent: 430m ***Grading:*** Moderate
Access Restrictions: RTÉ NL access road and
surrounding private land ***Map:*** OSi Sheet 16.

Start/Finish: the gated entrance to the RTÉ NL access road at **G:744:468**, 1.6km west-southwest of the CHPs. There is space on the grass verge for one car to park beside the public road a short distance south of the entrance. Do not block the gated entrances to the access road or any other properties. Do not enter the access road with a motor vehicle even if the gate is open. In-car satnav coordinates for the RTÉ NL access road entrance are: (a) **N54°22'10.03", W8°23'41.13"** or (b) **N54.369453°, W8.394758°**.

Route Description

(1) Gated entrance to RTÉ NL access road (G:74391:46825:221)

There is no gap or stile but the oddly shaped entrance gates can be climbed at their ladder-like hinged ends – requires care. Follow the access road uphill to where it meets the locked gate of the RTÉ NL compound. Follow the perimeter fence of the compound in either direction to arrive at the trig pillar – the CHP of Sligo.

(2) Truskmore summit (G:75893:47341:647)
Retrace your steps to (1).

OPTION A: Extension to the CHP of Leitrim from (2)
Important: read Special Note below. Proceed past the RTÉ NL compound on a grid bearing of 120° for 480m. Under no circumstances should you deviate from this course. Arrive at the cairn marking the CHP of Leitrim.

(3) Cairn at Truskmore Southeast Slope (G:76312:47096:631)
Return to the RTÉ NL access road along a grid bearing of 270° for 230m. Turn left onto the access road and follow it back down to the start point.

Option A adds 0.6km of horizontal distance and up to 10 minutes to the route. It also increases the vertical ascent by 10m.

Special Note:
The cairn marking the CHP of Leitrim lies on private agricultural land. Anyone planning to visit its location is advised to seek permission in advance from the relevant landowner.

Trig pillar marking the County High Point of Sligo at Truskmore summit

10. COUNTY
LEITRIM

Leitrim is a coastal county in the northwest of Ireland. With an area of 1,589km², it is the twenty-sixth largest county in Ireland and the smallest in Connacht. It shares land boundaries with six other counties: Roscommon, Sligo, Donegal, Fermanagh, Cavan and Longford.

Notable Geographical Facts about Leitrim

Leitrim is number 19 on the Irish county height rankings.
It is one of two counties in Ireland whose CHP lies on a slope rather than a summit (the other being Roscommon).
Leitrim is the most easterly county in Connacht.
At high tide, Leitrim becomes the most northerly county in mainland Connacht (Sligo holds this honour if we include islands) and at low tide, is the most northerly county in the province as a whole at approximately **G:787:587** just north of Tullaghan.

Truskmore Southeast Slope

A stone cairn on the upper southeast slope of Truskmore marks the sloped CHP of Leitrim at **G:76312:47096:631**. The CHP of Leitrim has been included as an extension to Walk 9 – Truskmore.
It is worth noting that the highest unshared summit lying entirely within Leitrim is that of Tievebaun Mountain at **G:768:499**. Its 611m summit is located in the Dartry Mountains 2.9km to the north of the CHP.

County Leitrim

11. COUNTY
ROSCOMMON

Roscommon is a landlocked county in the west of Ireland. With an area of 2,548km², it is the eleventh largest county in Ireland and the third largest in Connacht. It shares boundaries with seven other counties: Galway, Mayo, Sligo, Leitrim, Longford, Westmeath and Offaly.

Notable Geographical Facts about Roscommon

Roscommon is number 27 on the Irish county height rankings.

It is one of two counties in Ireland whose CHP lies on a slope rather than a summit (the other being Leitrim).

Roscommon is the only landlocked county in Connacht.

The geographical centre of Ireland (**M:924:418**) is in Roscommon, 11.6km to the west of Athlone.

The County Low Point of Roscommon is approximately 37m above mean sea level, giving. Roscommon a county height of 375m.

It is worth noting that the highest summit in Roscommon is that of Kilronan Mountain at **G:901:149**. Its 335m unshared summit is located in the Arigna Mountains 4.6km to the south of the CHP.

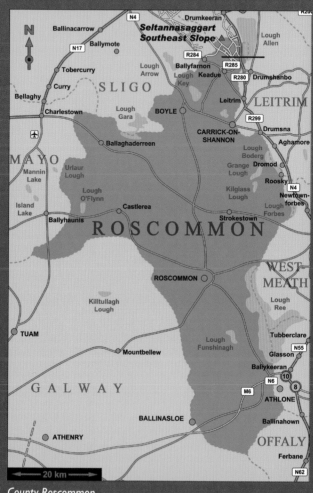

County Roscommon

SELTANNASAGGART SOUTHEAST SLOPE

A small stone cairn on the upper southeastern slopes of Seltannasaggart marks the sloped CHP of Roscommon at **G:904:195**. At 412m above sea level, this cairn is just on the Roscommon side of the county boundary with Leitrim in the Arigna Mountains. Seltannasaggart Southeast Slope is the most easterly CHP in Connacht. Seltannasaggart is often referred to as 'Corrie Mountain' or 'Corry Mountain'.

Seltannasaggart Southeast Slope lies 4.8km south of Drumkeeran, 7km north-northeast of Ballyfarnon and 11.2km northwest of Drumshanbo. Any of these locations would make a suitable base for exploring Seltannasaggart Southeast Slope, the Arigna Mountains and the surrounding area.

Route Summary

This out-and-back route follows part of the waymarked Miners Way. It starts in neighbouring Leitrim and follows a clearly marked track to a working sandpit surrounded by wind turbines. Only in the final 100m does the route enter Roscommon.

Seltannasaggart viewed from the south

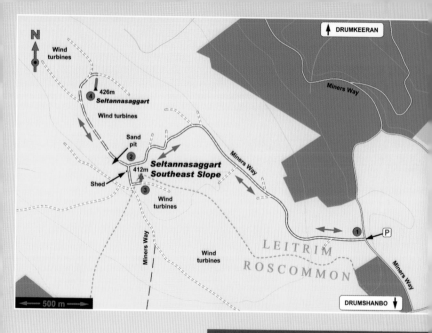

Time: 1 to 2 hours **Distance:** 4.9km
Ascent: 120m **Grading:** Easy
Access Restrictions: None identified, although a working quarry
and a wind farm are located very close by.
Maps: OSi Sheet 26; OSNI Sheet 26.

Start/Finish: the waymarked junction on the Miners Way at **G:920:191**,
1.6km east-southeast of the CHP. Up to two cars can park on the roadside. In-car
satnav coordinates for the start/finish are: (a) **N54°07'16.37", W8°07'24.29"**
or (b) **N54.121214°, W8.123414°**.

Route Description

(1) Start point at Miners Way junction (G:91979:19128:305)

Follow the stony track west uphill towards the wind farm. Avoid all side tracks.
Arrive at a track junction with sandpit workings directly ahead and to the right.

(2) Track junction near quarry (G:90305:19607:417)

Turn left to follow track southwards. Pass an industrial building on the right. Take
the next track to the left and follow for a short distance. A small cairn in the
heather to the left of the track marks the CHP of Roscommon.

(3) Cairn at Seltannasaggart Southeast Slope (G:90414:19521:412)

Retrace your steps to (1).

OPTION A: Out-and-back extension to Seltannasaggart summit from (2)

From (2), head north-northwest past the sandpit workings. Continue through a gate and into Corrie Mountain Wind Farm. Keep right at two junctions as the track curves right and towards the east. Continue along the track for 130m, then turn right towards the south-southwest. Arrive at the cairn marking the summit of Seltannasaggart.

(4) Seltannasaggart summit (G:90169:20112:426)

Retrace your steps back to the start point via (2).

Option A adds 1.9km of horizontal distance and up to 40 minutes to the route. It increases the vertical ascent by 20m.

Cairn marking the County High Point of Roscommon at Seltannasaggart Southeast Slope

ULSTER

Covering the northern quarter of Ireland, the province of Ulster comprises the nine counties of Down, Donegal, Derry, Tyrone, Cavan, Fermanagh, Armagh, Antrim and Monaghan. With an area of 22,175km², Ulster is the second largest of Ireland's four provinces. Notable mountain ranges include the Mournes, the Sperrins, the Derryveaghs, and the Bluestacks. The Provincial High Point of Ulster is Slieve Donard in Down (chapter 12).

The Mourne Mountains from the northwest

12. COUNTY
DOWN

Down is a coastal county in the northeast of Ireland. With an area of 2,496km², it is the twelfth largest county in Ireland and the fourth largest in Ulster. It shares land boundaries with two other counties: Armagh and Antrim.

Notable Geographical Facts about Down

Down is number 5 on the Irish county height rankings.
It is the most easterly county in Ireland and also the most southerly county in Northern Ireland.

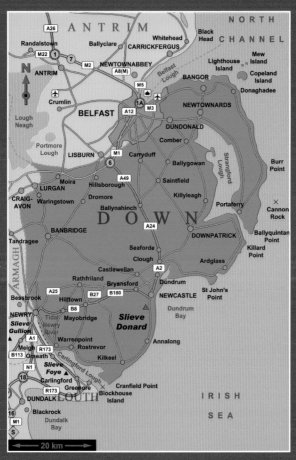

County Down

SLIEVE DONARD

The large stone cairn at the 850m summit of Slieve Donard marks the natural CHP of Down at **J:35802:27693:850**, while the trig pillar atop the stone tower nearby marks the man-made CHP at **J:35789:27687:853**. The choice of cairn or trig pillar is entirely up to you, and both qualify equally. This summit in the Mourne Mountains is classed as a Hewitt, a Marilyn and a Vandeleur-Lynam. It is the Provincial High Point of Ulster and the highest point in Northern Ireland. It is also the most easterly CHP in Ireland.

Slieve Donard summit is 3.9km south-southwest of Newcastle, 5.4km south-south-east of Bryansford and 8.1km north of Annalong. Any of these locations would make a suitable base for exploring Slieve Donard, the Mourne Mountains and the surrounding area.

Slieve Donard viewed from Newcastle

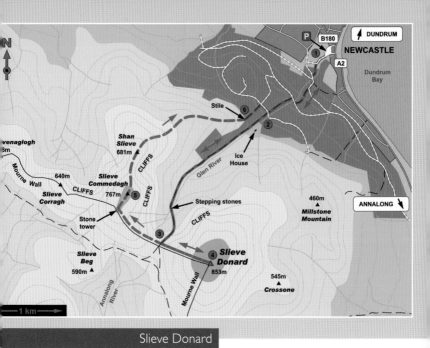

Slieve Donard

Route Summary

This out-and-back route is the most popular approach to Slieve Donard summit. Starting from the town of Newcastle, it follows forest and mountain paths alongside the Glen River before a steep ascent along the Mourne Wall. There is an option to include neighbouring Slieve Commedagh – the second highest summit in Ulster. Mostly follows clear paths along linear features, although the Slieve Commedagh option requires good navigation skills in poor visibility.

Time: 3½ to 5 hours ***Distance:*** 9.5km
Ascent: 850m ***Grading:*** Moderate
Access Restrictions: None
Maps: OSNI Sheet 29; OSNI *Mournes Activity Map.*

Start/Finish: Donard Park at **J:374:306**. This is at the southern end of Newcastle and is 3.3km north-northeast of the CHP. Donard Park has substantial car parking space, public toilets and allows easy access to nearby shops, pubs and restaurants in the town. In-car satnav coordinates for Donard Park are: (a) **N54°12'20.79", W5°53'40.34"** or (b) **N54.205775°, W5.894539°**.

Route Description

(1) Donard Park (J:37429:30582:005)

From the car park, head southwest along a tarmac road towards grassy parkland. Ignore a side road to the left. When the tarmac road bends right, take a gravel track to the left along the edge of the grassy area. Enter Donard Forest and proceed uphill. Keep to the right of the Glen River. Turn left onto a gravel forest track across a bridge. Turn right immediately along a cobbly track on the left side of the river. Where the track disappears, follow a well-worn path southwest beside the river to intercept a second forest track. Turn right along the track and across a bridge. Turn left immediately up a path through the trees. Follow the right side of the river to arrive at a third forest track.

(2) Edge of Donard Forest (J:36587:29721:188)

Note the bridge to the left if planning to do Option A. Ignore for now, and continue straight across the track along a path and out of the forest. Keep the Glen River to your left. The forest continues for a while on your right. Continue along a clear path through open mountain terrain. Cross the river at stepping stones and ascend a steep section of well-made stone path to arrive at the Mourne Wall.

(3) Col between Donard and Commedagh (J:34991:27945:583)

Turn left and ascend steeply along the Mourne Wall towards the east-southeast. Keep to the left-hand side of the wall where a stone path has been built to minimise erosion. Arrive at Slieve Donard summit. The natural CHP of Down is underneath the large summit cairn, and the man-made CHP is at the top of the roof-mounted trig point at the corner of the Mourne Wall.

Glen River track

Trig pillar and cairn marking the man-made and natural County High Points of Down at Slieve Donard summit

(4) Slieve Donard summit (J:35789:27687:853)
Retrace your steps to (1).

OPTION A: Alternative descent from (3) to (2) via Slieve Commedagh
From (3), follow the Mourne Wall west-northwest. Arrive at a stone tower marking the highest point where the wall passes over Slieve Commedagh. Turn right here, and head north-northeast to the cairn marking the summit of Slieve Commedagh.

(5) Slieve Commedagh summit (J:34613:28623:767)
Descend northwards off Slieve Commedagh. Beware of the cliffs on the right dropping down into the Pot of Pulgarve. Follow the path close to the cliff top to Shan Slieve. Descend northeast along the Slievenamaddy spur to arrive at a stile on the edge of the forest.

(6) Stile at forest perimeter (J:36238:29648:268)
Cross the stile and follow a path down through the forest. Arrive at a crossroads of forest tracks and paths. Turn right along the track and follow to the bridge at (2). Turn left before the bridge, and retrace your steps to (1) along the Glen River.

Option A adds 1.5km of horizontal distance and up to 1 hour to the descent. It also increases the vertical ascent by 190m.

Special Note:
Extra care needs to be taken along the Shan Slieve ridge during strong crosswinds.

13. COUNTY
DONEGAL

Donegal is a coastal county in the northwest corner of Ireland. With an area of 4,843km², it is the fourth largest county in Ireland and the largest in Ulster. It shares land boundaries with four other counties: Derry, Tyrone, Fermanagh and Leitrim.

Notable Geographical Facts about Donegal

Donegal is number 11 on the Irish county height rankings.
It is the most northerly county in Ireland and the most westerly county in Ulster.

County Donegal

ERRIGAL MOUNTAIN

The unfurnished 751m summit of Errigal Mountain is the CHP of Donegal at **B:928:208**. The summit area comprises two distinct peaks which are 60m apart and linked by a narrow ridge called One Man's Path – care is required in strong crosswinds. The southwest peak is the actual summit and is the first of the two to be reached if following the route described in this book. OSi maps indicate the presence of a triangulation station at the summit, but there is no evidence of a trig pillar on Errigal Mountain. This summit in the Derryveagh Mountains is classed as a Hewitt, a Marilyn and a Vandeleur-Lynam. It is the most westerly CHP in Ulster.

The summit of Errigal Mountain is 1.4km northeast of Money More/ Dunlewey, 11.3km south of Falcarragh and 12.4km east-southeast of Bunbeg/ Derrybeg. Any of these locations would make a suitable base for exploring Errigal, the Derryveagh Mountains and the surrounding area.

Route Summary

This out-and-back initially crosses some potentially very boggy ground before ascending on to a rocky ridge leading to the twin-peaked summit of Errigal Mountain. Much of the ascent is on a clear path over loose rocks and scree. The optional descent route described includes a visit to Mackoght, which is often referred to as 'Wee Errigal'.

Errigal Mountain from the west

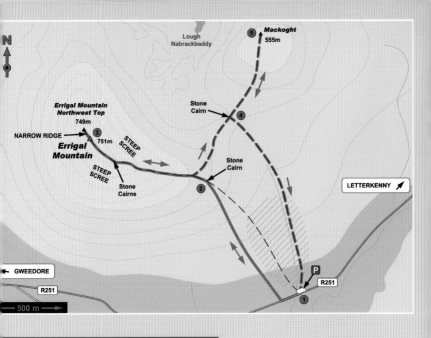

Errigal Mountain

Time: 1½ to 3 hours ***Distance:*** 4.4km
Ascent: 530m ***Grading:*** Moderate
Access Restrictions: None ***Map:*** OSi Sheet 1.

Start/Finish: the car park beside the R251 at **B:943:197**, 1.8km southeast of the CHP. In-car satnav coordinates for the start/finish are: (a) **N55°01'29.86", W8°05'24.38"** or (b) **N55.024961°, W8.090106°**.

Route Description

(1) Car park beside R251 (B:94285:19729:226)

If visibility is good, the ridge path on Errigal Mountain can be seen clearly northwest of the start point. Instead of taking the most obvious direct route to it, turn right out of the car park and follow the R251 downhill towards the west-southwest for about 100m. Then turn right and head north-northwest along a route which should be drier than the more direct approach. The ground gets steeper and drier until you arrive at a cairn marking the start of the ridge path.

(2) Cairn at start of ridge (B:93558:20504:516)

From here, an obvious path leads all the way to the summit of Errigal Mountain. This is a stony path and loose pieces are likely to move underfoot on some sections. Pass a walled cairn marking the start of the most exposed part of the ridge. Follow the well-worn path to arrive at the unmarked CHP of Donegal. The ridge continues beyond the CHP towards Errigal Mountain's Northwest Top. If you wish, you can make the short out-and-back excursion along One Man's Path to visit this slightly lower peak.

(3) Errigal Mountain summit (B:92824:20774:751)
Retrace your steps to (I).

Special Note:
Extra care needs to be taken on Errigal Mountain's summit and ridge in strong winds.

OPTION A: Alternative descent from (2) to (I) via Mackoght
At (2), keep on the high line of the ridge. Follow the ridge as it curves left towards the northeast. Arrive at a tall, square-based cairn at the col.

(4) Col cairn (B:93826:20907:404)
Continue straight through the col towards the northeast. Keep this general heading, and pick your own route through the rocks to arrive at Mackoght summit.

(5) Mackoght summit (B:94016:21473:555)
Retrace your steps back down to (4). Turn left at the cairn and head south-southeast. Pick up the stream and follow it to the car park. You are likely to encounter soft ground here.

Option A adds 1.9km of horizontal distance and up to I hour to the descent. It also increases the vertical ascent by 150m.

Looking back across One Man's Path from Errigal's Northwest Top towards the unmarked County High Point of Donegal

14. COUNTY
DERRY

Also known as Londonderry, Derry is a coastal county in the north of Ireland. With an area of 2,110km², it is the fifteenth largest county in Ireland and the fifth largest in Ulster. It shares land boundaries with three other counties: Antrim, Tyrone and Donegal.

Notable Geographical Facts about Derry

Derry is number 14 on the Irish county height rankings.

The largest coastal plain in Ireland is in Derry. Including the Magilligan Lowlands and the Roe Estuary, this covers an area of approximately 60km² of land lying below the 10m contour between the cliffs of Binevenagh and Lough Foyle.

Sawel Mountain

The trig pillar on Sawel Mountain summit marks the shared CHP of Derry and neighbouring Tyrone. Refer to Chapter 15 – County Tyrone – for information about Sawel Mountain and its walking route description.

The highest unshared summit lying entirely within Derry is that of Spelhoagh at **H:708:979**. Its 568m summit is located in the Sperrin Mountains 9km to the east of the CHP.

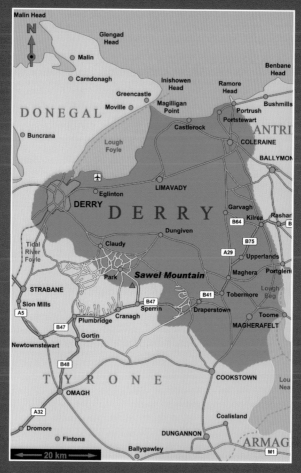

County Derry

15. COUNTY
TYRONE

Tyrone is a landlocked county in the north of Ireland. With an area of 3,213km², it is the seventh largest county in Ireland, the second largest in Ulster and the largest in Northern Ireland. It shares land boundaries with five other counties: Derry, Armagh, Monaghan, Fermanagh and Donegal.

Notable Geographical Facts about Tyrone

Tyrone is number 15 on the Irish county height rankings.

The geographical centre of Ulster **(H:572:737)** is in Tyrone, 4.5km west-northwest of the village of Carrickmore.

The geographical centre of Northern Ireland **(H:785:813)** is in Tyrone 4.1km northwest of the town of Cookstown.

The County Low Point of Tyrone is at an elevation of approximately 2m above mean sea level.

The highest unshared summit lying entirely within Tyrone is that of Mullaghclogha at **H:557:957**. Its 635m summit is located 6.3km to the west-southwest of the CHP.

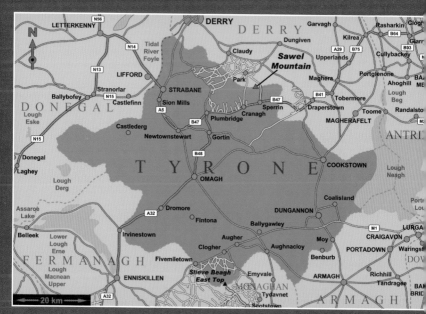

County Tyrone

SAWEL MOUNTAIN

The trig pillar on the small stony mound at the 678m summit of Sawel Mountain marks the shared CHP of Derry and Tyrone at **H:618:973**. A post-and-wire fence passes to within about 10m of the trig pillar, and it was once believed that this fence marked the Derry/Tyrone boundary. OSNI has confirmed that this is not the case and that the undefined county boundary passes through the Sawel Mountain trig pillar. This summit in the Sperrin Mountains is classed as a Hewitt, a Marilyn and a Vandeleur-Lynam.

Sawel Mountain summit is 5.7km south-southeast of Park, 14.7km east-northeast of Plumbridge and 16.7km west of Draperstown. Any of these locations would make a suitable base for exploring Sawel Mountain, the Sperrin Mountains and the surrounding area.

Route Summary

This out-and-back route roughly follows the Derry/Tyrone county boundary from the highest point on Sperrin Road. The route is clearly marked by a fence along its entire length. Expect to encounter very boggy sections, especially in the lower half of the route.

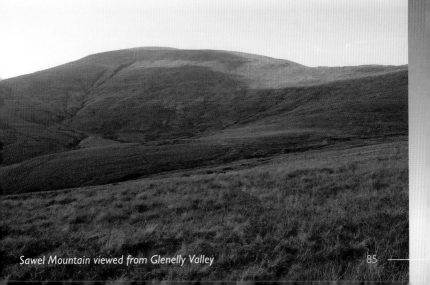

Sawel Mountain viewed from Glenelly Valley

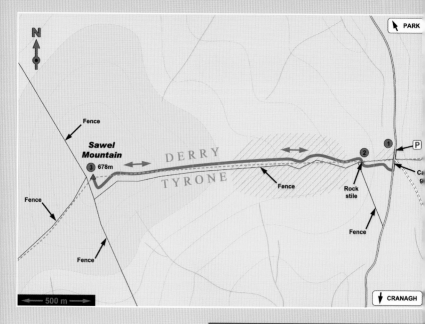

Time: 1½ to 2½ hours **Distance:** 4.6km
Ascent: 350m **Grading:** Moderate
Access Restrictions: None identified, although nearby landowners are known to have objected to walkers crossing their land in recent years
Maps: OSNI Sheet 13; OSNI *Sperrins Activity Map*.

Start/Finish: at **H:639:976**, the high point of Sperrin Road where there is roadside parking for up to three cars. This is 2.1km east of the CHP. In-car satnav coordinates for the start/finish are: (a) **N54°49'18.89", W7°00'23.50"** or (b) **N54.821914°, W7.006528°**.

Route Description

(1) Parking spot on Sperrin Road (H:63907:97574:338)

Turn left and head south along Sperrin Road for about 100m. Cross a cattle grid and turn right into the field immediately. Veer right, taking the driest route to intercept the fence heading uphill. Follow the fence westwards and ascend a short steep section. Just before arriving at a fence junction, locate the two rocks (one on each side of the fence) which can be used as a stile.

(2) Rock stile (H:63671:97448:371)

Cross the fence by making use of the two rocks, and continue westwards. No further fence crossings are required on the rest of the ascent. The ground becomes less steep, but becomes boggy. It may be necessary to bypass some

Cross fence using these rocks as a handy stile

soft channels which are too wide to cross. Stay as close to the fence as possible, keeping it to your left. The ground gets steeper again, and conditions underfoot improve as you ascend. Continue along the fence as it veers left and then levels out. The summit is now a short distance to your right, but keep to the fence for guidance. The fence bends sharply to the right at a junction. Turn right and follow the fence north-northwest until the trig pillar comes into view. Veer right to arrive at the trig pillar – the shared CHP of Derry and Tyrone.

(3) Sawel Mountain summit (H:61796:97303:678)
Retrace your steps to (1).

Trig pillar marking the shared County High Point of Tyrone and Derry at Sawel Mountain summit

16. COUNTY
FERMANAGH

Fermanagh is a landlocked county in the northwest of Ireland. With an area of 1,875km², it is the twentieth largest county in Ireland and the seventh largest in Ulster. It shares boundaries with five other counties: Donegal, Tyrone, Monaghan, Cavan and Leitrim.

Notable Geographical Facts about Fermanagh

Fermanagh is number 16 on the Irish county height rankings.
The County Low Point of Fermanagh is approximately 25m above mean sea level.
Fermanagh has a county height of 641m. It is the most westerly county in Northern Ireland.

Cuilcagh

The trig pillar on Cuilcagh summit marks the shared CHP of Fermanagh and neighbouring Cavan. Refer to Chapter 17 – County Cavan – for information about Cuilcagh and its walking route description.
The highest unshared summit lying entirely within Fermanagh is that of Mullaleam at **H:153:319**. Its 424m summit is located in the Cuilcagh Mountains 4.9km to the northeast of the CHP.

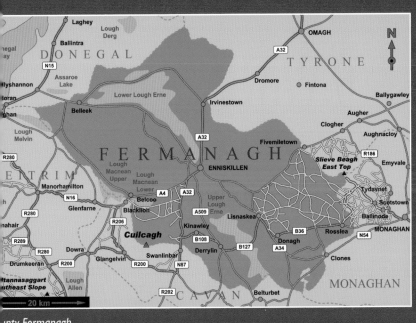

County Fermanagh

17. COUNTY
CAVAN

Cavan is a landlocked county in the north midlands of Ireland. With an area of 1,932km², it is the nineteenth largest county in Ireland and the sixth largest in Ulster. It shares boundaries with six other counties: Fermanagh, Monaghan, Meath, Westmeath, Longford and Leitrim.

Notable Geographical Facts about Cavan

Cavan is number 17 on the Irish county height rankings.

The County Low Point of Cavan is approximately 32m above mean sea level.

Cavan has a county height of 634m.

It is the most southerly county in Ulster.

The highest unshared summit lying entirely within Cavan is that of Slievenakilla at **H:033:257**. Its 543m summit is located in the Iron Mountains 9.3km to the west-southwest of the CHP.

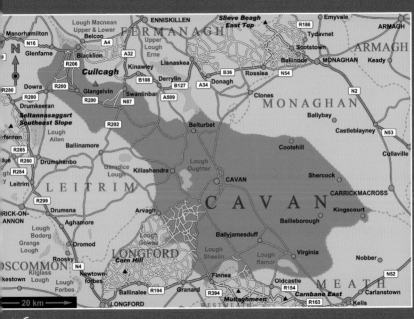

County Cavan

CUILCAGH

The trig pillar on top of the large stone cairn at the 665m summit of Cuilcagh marks the shared CHP of Fermanagh and Cavan at **H:123:280**. This summit in the Cuilcagh Mountains is classed as a Hewitt, a Marilyn and a Vandeleur-Lynam. It has the added distinction of being the highest point on the border between the Republic of Ireland and Northern Ireland.

Cuilcagh summit is 6.9km west of Swanlinbar, 11km south-southeast of Blacklion/Belcoo and 13.2km east of Dowra. Any of these locations would make a suitable base for exploring Cuilcagh, the Cuilcagh Mountains and the surrounding area.

Route Summary

This out-and-back route initially passes through a Coillte forest along an access track leading to a small telecommunications mast. The remainder of the route follows faint paths along a broad ridge, and crosses potentially boggy ground.

Time: 2½ to 5 hours **Distance:** 10.8km
Ascent: 390m **Grading:** Moderate
Access Restrictions: None identified
Maps: OSi Sheet 26; OSNI Sheet 26

Cuilcagh viewed from Benbeg

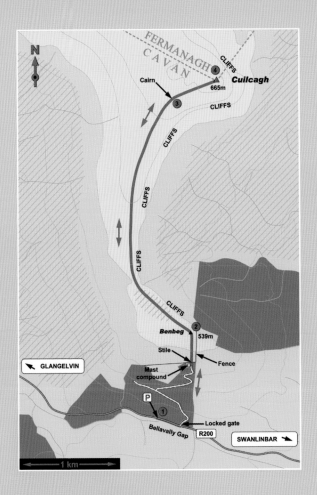

Start/Finish: at **H:117:246** at a roadside parking spot on the R200 between Swanlinbar and Glangelvin. This is 3.5km south of the CHP. In-car satnav coordinates for the start/finish are: (a) **N54°10'11.80", W7°49'18.05"** or (b) **N54.169944°, W7.821681°**.

Cairn marking the route to Cuilcagh

Route Description

(1) Roadside parking spot at Bellavally Gap (H:11695:24560:330)
Follow the road east towards its highest point. After about 250m, arrive at the gated entrance to a track on the left. Take this track and follow its zig-zagging route uphill through the Coillte forest. Avoid straight options at junctions to arrive at the telecommunications mast compound. Continue straight past the compound, keeping it to your left. The ground is likely to be soft here. Cross the fence using the stile provided. Continue straight towards the north and roughly parallel to a fence on your right. Arrive at the summit of Benbeg.

(2) Benbeg summit (H:12064:25437:539)
Head northwest along a faint path through boggy terrain keeping close to the right-hand side of this broad ridge. The ground falls away steeply on the right, and the ridge curves northwards. If the path becomes unclear, veer left along the high line of the ridge to avoid the cliffs. Make a grassy ascent onto Cuilcagh plateau.

(3) Cairn on Cuilcagh plateau (H:11938:27837:647)
If visibility is good, the summit can easily be identified from here. Head east-northeast to arrive at the large cairn and trig pillar – the shared CHP of Fermanagh and Cavan.

(4) Cuilcagh summit (H:12354:28011:665)
Retrace your steps to (1).

Trig pillar marking the shared County High Point of Cavan and Fermanagh at Cuilcagh summit

18. COUNTY
ARMAGH

Armagh is a landlocked county in the northeast of Ireland. With an area of 1,300km², it is the twenty-seventh largest county in Ireland, the eighth largest in Ulster and the smallest in Northern Ireland. It shares land boundaries with four other counties: Down, Monaghan, Tyrone and Louth.

Notable Geographical Facts about Armagh

Armagh is number 21 on the Irish county height rankings.

It is one of five landlocked counties in Ireland connected to the sea by tidal river estuaries.

The County Low Point of Armagh is at sea level along the estuary of the Newry River. As its County Low Point experiences the full tidal range, it could be argued that Armagh should be classed as a coastal county.

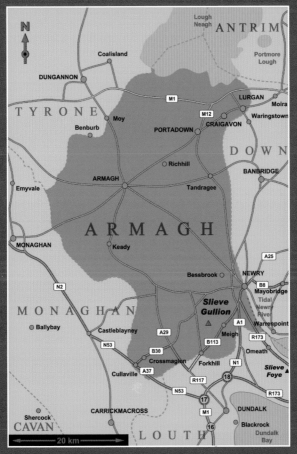

County Armagh

SLIEVE GULLION

The trig pillar on top of the large stone cairn at the 573m summit of Slieve Gullion marks the CHP of Armagh at **J:025:203**. The stone cairn beneath the trig pillar houses the highest surviving passage tomb so far discovered in Ireland – this can easily be entered from the side of the cairn. The summit area has an orientation panel identifying various places which may be visible from the summit, depending on the weather conditions. This summit in the Ring of Gullion is classed as a Marilyn and is the most southerly CHP in Ulster.

Slieve Gullion summit is 2.8km west of Meigh, 4.7km north-northeast of Forkhill and 8.5km southwest of Newry. Any of these locations would make a suitable base for exploring Slieve Gullion, the Ring of Gullion and the surrounding area.

Slieve Gullion viewed from the east

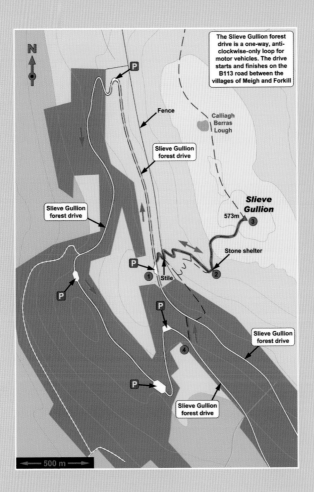

The Slieve Gullion forest drive is a one-way, anti-clockwise-only loop for motor vehicles. The drive starts and finishes on the B113 road between the villages of Meigh and Forkill

Fence

Calliagh Berras Lough

Slieve Gullion forest drive

Slieve Gullion forest drive

Slieve Gullion

573m ③

Stone shelter

② Stile

Slieve Gullion forest drive

Slieve Gullion forest drive

← 500 m →

N

Slieve Gullion

Route Summary

An out-and-back route which begins with a distinct path through heather and grass but becomes progressively steeper and more rugged towards the summit. An optional forest loop is also included.

Stone shelter at (2)

Time: ¾ to 1½ hours **Distance:** 2.4km
Ascent: 220m **Grading:** Moderate
Access Restrictions: None
Maps: OSNI Sheet 29; OSi Sheet 36.

Start/Finish: at **J:018:200** at the car park on the one-way anticlockwise Slieve Gullion forest drive. This is 720m west-southwest of the CHP. The forest drive is accessed via the main entrance to Slieve Gullion Forest Park at **J:043:191**. In-car satnav coordinates for the forest park entrance are: (a) **N54°06'36.54", W6°24'19.31"** or (b) **N54.110150°, W6.405364°**.

Route Description

(1) Start point (J:01820:20031:361)

From the car park, turn left and proceed along the forest drive for a short distance. Take the well-worn path to the right (this may be marked by a post) and follow uphill to arrive at a fence. Cross at the stile and continue along the zig-zagging path to a stone shelter with an information panel inside.

(2) Stone shelter (J:02221:20012:451)

Follow the path as it continues uphill past the left-hand side of the stone shelter. The path becomes steeper and rougher from this point. Arrive at the trig point – the CHP of Armagh.

(3) Slieve Gullion summit (J:02482:20337:573)

Retrace your steps to (1). When passing (2) on the descent, take the path forking to the right. If you take the wrong path you will descend to arrive at a point on the fence where there is no stile. In this case, follow the fence to the right until you arrive at the stile. Cross the stile and descend along the path to the start point.

OPTION A: Additional looped section from (1)

From the car park, turn left along the forest drive route. Follow this all the way round to (4) avoiding all turn-offs.

(4) Start of path (J:02067:19508:302)

Turn left and follow the path uphill to meet the road. Turn left along the road to arrive at the car park.

Option A adds 5.5km of horizontal distance and up to 2 hours to the route. It also increases the vertical ascent by 200m.

The County High Points of Down and Louth from the County High Point of Armagh at Slieve Gullion summit

19. COUNTY
ANTRIM

Antrim is a coastal county in the northeast corner of Ireland. With an area of 3,111km², it is the ninth largest county in Ireland and the third largest in Ulster. It shares land boundaries with two other counties: Down and Derry.

Notable Geographical Facts about Antrim

Antrim is number 22 on the Irish county height rankings.
It is the most northerly county in Northern Ireland.
The shortest distance between Ireland and Great Britain is just 20.1km, from Torr Head **(D:235:408)** in Antrim to the Mull of Kintyre **(D:398:525)** in Scotland.

County Antrim

TROSTAN

The trig pillar on top of the large earth and stone cairn at the 550m summit of Trostan marks the CHP of Antrim at **D:179:236**. This summit in the Antrim Hills is classed as a Marilyn and is the most northerly CHP in Ireland, beating Errigal Mountain in Donegal by just 2.8km.

Trostan summit is 7.5km west-southwest of Cushendall, 11.5km southwest of Cushendun and 12.3km northeast of Clogh. Any of these locations would make a suitable base for exploring Trostan, the Antrim Hills and the surrounding area.

Trostan viewed from the start point

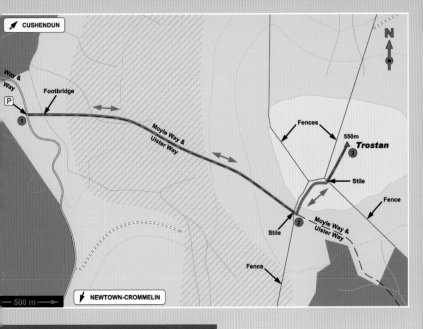

N

Way & Way

Footbridge

P

① Moyle Way & Ulster Way

Fences

550m Trostan ③

Stile

Fence

② Moyle Way & Ulster Way

Stile

Fence

— 500 m —→

Trostan

Route Summary

This out-and-back route mainly follows the waymarked Moyle Way – a quality section of the Ulster Way. The first half of the walk crosses featureless, boggy terrain. Although this route is mainly waymarked by posts, navigation skills may be required in very poor visibility.

Time: 1½ to 2½ hours **Distance:** 5.5km
Ascent: 230m **Grading:** Moderate
Access Restrictions: None
Maps: OSNI Sheet 9; OSNI *Glens of Antrim Activity Map*.

Start/Finish: On the minor road between Newtown-Crommelin and Cushendun at **D:157:238** where there is roadside parking for up to two cars. This location is marked by an information panel and Moyle Way/Ulster Way signs, and is 2.3km west of the CHP. In-car satnav coordinates for the start/finish are: (a) **N55°02'53.67", W6°11'28.11"** or (b) **N55.048242°, W6.191142°**.

Route Description

(1) Start point (D:15663:23814:329)

From the road, head east towards Trostan summit. Cross the footbridge and follow all waymarkers. Ground can become quite boggy along this section. The markers guide you gradually onto a southeasterly course until you arrive at a fence with a stile.

(2) Leave Moyle Way at stile (D:17564:23139:497)

Cross the fence using the stile. Take an immediate left after crossing to leave the waymarked Moyle Way. Follow the fence north-northeast. Continue along the fence as it bends right. Arrive at another stile. Turn left here, and cross the fence. Continue northeast past a small cairn to arrive at the large summit cairn and trig pillar – the CHP of Antrim.

(3) Trostan summit (D:17960:23596:550)

Retrace your steps to (1).

Trig pillar marking the County High Point of Antrim at Trostan summit

20. COUNTY
MONAGHAN

Monaghan is a landlocked county in the north midlands of Ireland. With an area of 1,295km², it is the twenty-eighth largest county in Ireland and the smallest in Ulster. It shares boundaries with six other counties: Cavan, Fermanagh, Tyrone, Armagh, Louth and Meath.

Notable Geographical Facts about Monaghan
Monaghan is number 29 on the Irish county height rankings.
The County Low Point of Monaghan is approximately 22m above mean sea level, the lowest of the nine landlocked counties in Ireland not connected to the sea by tidal river estuaries.
Monaghan has a county height of 351m.

County Monaghan

SLIEVE BEAGH EAST TOP

An unmarked natural mound at the 373m summit of Slieve Beagh East Top is the CHP of Monaghan at **H:532:436**.

Slieve Beagh East Top is 8.4km south of Clogher, 9.6km east-southeast of Fivemiletown and 10.2km northwest of Scotstown. Any of these locations would make a suitable base for exploring Slieve Beagh East Top and the surrounding area.

Route Description

This out-and-back route starts along a stone track before entering a bleak and featureless landscape. The Slieve Beagh plateau is an expansive area of upland blanket bog where soft ground can make walking very difficult. Navigation is also an issue due to a lack of visual landmarks on the plateau.

Time: 1¼ to 2¾ hours ***Distance:*** 6.3km
Ascent: 120m ***Grading:*** Moderate
Access Restrictions: None
Maps: OSi Sheet 28A; OSNI Sheet 18.

Continue straight across the bog from this track junction at (2)

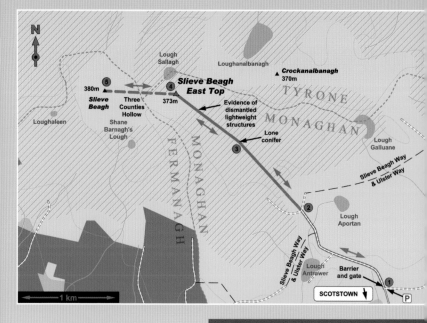

Slieve Beagh East Top

Start/Finish: at **H:554:416** where a cul-de-sac road ends, 3km southeast of the CHP. It is possible to park on an obvious concrete surface just to the right of where the road ends at a gate. The cul-de-sac road is signposted as 'Three County Hollow' at **H:571:404**. In-car satnav coordinates for the start/finish are: (a) **N54°19'12.15", W7°08'58.11"** or (b) **N54.320042°, W7.149475°**.

Route Description

(1) Electric gate at end of cul-de-sac (H:55395:41587:264)

Pass through the pedestrian gate beside the electric barrier to access the track. Ignore a side track and the waymarked Slieve Beagh Way path to the left. Arrive at a fork in the track.

(2) Track junction (H:54531:42364:313)

Ignore both the left and right tracks and continue straight ahead past the Slieve Beagh Way marker post. Ascend the slope and enter a vast open area of blanket bog. If visibility is good, a lone conifer will come into view on the horizon. Aim for this. (If visibility is poor, follow a grid bearing of 317° from (2) for approximately 900m.)

(3) Lone conifer (H:53850:43084:360)

Continue straight past the conifer and over a shallow rise. On a clear day, Slieve Beagh East Top can be seen directly ahead. To the right of the CHP is Slieve Beagh summit in neighbouring Fermanagh. To the left of the CHP is a telecommunications mast in Tyrone. From (3), follow a grid bearing of 306° for approximately 850m.

Pass the remains of dismantled lightweight structures (possibly used to aid the drying of peat) to arrive at a small, unmarked mound – the CHP of Monaghan. A hole at the CHP suggests that there may have been a marker post here in the past.

(4) Slieve Beagh East Top (H:53177:43571:373)

Retrace your steps to (1). Initially follow a grid bearing of 126° from (4) to (3), then a grid bearing of 137° from (3) to rejoin the track at (2).

OPTION A: Out-and-back extension to Slieve Beagh summit from (4)

From (4), Slieve Beagh summit is the high point to the west. If visibility is good, head straight towards it. In poor visibility, follow a grid bearing of 274° for approximately 780m. On the way, you will cross the international boundary from the Republic of Ireland into Northern Ireland. In fact, you will probably set foot in three different counties within a period of one minute – Monaghan, Tyrone and Fermanagh. Arrive at Slieve Beagh summit.

(5) Slieve Beagh summit (H:52391:43634:380)

Return to (4) by retracing your steps along a grid bearing of 94°.

Option A adds 1.6km of horizontal distance and up to 1 hour to the route. It also increases the vertical ascent by 10m.

Special Note:

Slieve Beagh is a flat and featureless landscape. It is easy to get disorientated here and basic navigation skills are required, even in good conditions. Only hillwalkers with sound navigation experience should consider this walk when visibility is poor.

The unmarked County High Point of Monaghan at Slieve Beagh East Top

LEINSTER

Covering the southeastern quarter of Ireland, the province of Leinster comprises the twelve counties of Wicklow, Wexford, Carlow, Dublin, Louth, Offaly, Laois, Kilkenny, Kildare, Longford, Meath and Westmeath. With an area of 19,764km², Leinster is the third largest of Ireland's four provinces. Notable mountain ranges include the Wicklow Mountains, the Blackstairs Mountains, the Slieve Bloom Mountains, and the Cooley Mountains. The Provincial High Point of Leinster is Lugnaquillia Mountain in Wicklow (chapter 21).

Glen of Imaal in the Wicklow Mountains

WICKLOW

Wicklow is a coastal county in the southeast of Ireland. With an area of 2,024km², it is the seventeenth largest county in Ireland and the fourth largest in Leinster. It shares land boundaries with four other counties: Dublin, Wexford, Carlow and Kildare.

Notable Geographical Facts about Wicklow

Wicklow is number 2 on the Irish county height rankings.

Based on the distorted Irish Grid referencing system, Wicklow is the most easterly county in the Republic of Ireland. Based on more accurate latitude/longitude referencing, the easternmost point in the Republic as a whole is The Nose at **O:331:512** on Lambay Island in neighbouring Dublin.

Ireland's tallest waterfall is in Wicklow, the 121m-high Powerscourt Waterfall.

County Wicklow

LUGNAQUILLIA MOUNTAIN

The trig pillar on top of the stone cairn at the 925m summit of Lugnaquillia Mountain marks the CHP of Wicklow at **T:032:918**. This summit in the Wicklow Mountains is classed as a Hewitt, a Marilyn and a Vandeleur-Lynam. It has the added distinction of being the Provincial High Point of Leinster and Ireland's highest summit outside Kerry. Lugnaquillia Mountain is often incorrectly referred to as being a Munro – a classification reserved only for certain Scottish summits higher than 3,000 feet (914.4m) above sea level.

Lugnaquillia Mountain summit is 11.7km east-southeast of Donard, 12km west-southwest of Laragh and 16.8km east of Baltinglass. Any of these locations would make a suitable base for exploring Lugnaquillia Mountain, the Wicklow Mountains and the surrounding area.

Route Summary

This out-and-back route passes through the Glen of Imaal Artillery Range. Clear tracks at the start lead onto a waymarked path. There are some moderately steep sections, and the final ascent to the flat summit area is quite rocky. Cliffs drop sharply from the summit area into the North and South Prisons. Navigation skills are required, especially in poor visibility.

Time: 4 to 6½ hours **Distance:** 13.3km
Ascent: 730m **Grading:** Moderate
Access Restrictions: Part of the described route follows one of two recommended 'safe' routes through the Glen of Imaal Artillery Range.
The public are permitted to follow only these safe routes if passing through the range, and only when training exercises are not taking place. Red flags and red lights at entry points indicate that training is in progress on the range. Anyone planning to walk the route described below should contact the Glen of Imaal Army Warden in advance to check if training exercises are planned. The 24-hour telephone number is +353 (0) 45 404653. Alternatively, check the noticeboards dotted around the area – one is located in front of the Army Information & Advice Centre beside the start/finish.
Maps: OSi Sheet 56; Harvey Superwalker *Wicklow Mountains*; EastWest Mapping *Lugnaquilla & Glendalough*.

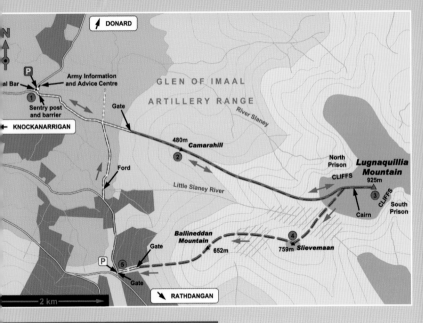

Lugnaquillia Mountain

Start/Finish: the car park of the Imaal Bar (Fenton's Pub) at **S:973:935**. This is 6.1km west-northwest of the CHP. In-car satnav coordinates for the Imaal Bar are: (a) **N52°59'00.70", W6°33'08.11"** or (b) **N52.983528°, W6.552253°**.

Route Description
(1) Start point at Imaal Bar (S:97285:93477:195)
From the car park, turn left along the road past the front of the Imaal Bar. Take an immediate left after the bar to follow a track. Pass the Michael Dwyer statue. Continue eastwards along the track to arrive at a red military notice. Turn right and follow the track south initially, keeping straight at all junctions. Arrive at a gate marking the end of the track. Pass through the smaller of the two gates, and follow the waymarkers uphill to arrive at the summit of Camarahill.

(2) Camarahill summit (S:99746:92471:480)
Continue straight over the summit towards the east-southeast as indicated by the waymarkers along the high line of this broad ridge. Arrive at the bottom of a moderately steep rocky section. Pick a route up this in a general east-northeast direction. Arrive on the flat summit area of Lugnaquillia Mountain. Head east to a small stone cairn. The CHP should now be in sight straight ahead. Continue east past the small cairn to arrive at the large summit cairn and trig pillar – the CHP of Wicklow.

(3) Lugnaquillia summit (T:03211:91779:925)
Retrace your steps to (1).

Army Information & Advice Centre beside the start point

*Lugnaquillia Mountain
viewed from Camarahill*

OPTION A: Alternative descent from (3) via Slievemaan

Retrace your steps westwards from the CHP. Pass the small cairn and veer left to find a path descending off the summit area towards the southwest. Follow this path. Cross the very boggy col between Lugnaquillia Mountain and Slievemaan. Continue straight ahead and follow the path to the summit of Slievemaan.

(4) Slievemaan summit (T:01755:90817:759)

Descend west along the path from Slievemaan summit. Cross another boggy col and continue up and over Ballineddan Mountain. Keep to this path as it zig-zags down to meet a gate. Pass through the gate and follow the track down to the road.

(5) Gated track entrance (S:98668:90378:309)

Cross the gate, and turn right along the road and follow it north for approximately 1.5km. Turn right along a track where a red military sign is displayed at the junction. Follow this track north and cross the Little Slaney River at a ford – beware of slippery rocks. Arrive at a crossroads of tracks – you passed this point on the ascent. Turn left and follow the track to the Michael Dwyer statue. Turn right past the Imaal Bar to the car park.

Option A adds 2.6km of horizontal distance and up to 90 minutes to the route. It also increases the vertical ascent by 90m.

Trig pillar marking the County High Point of Wicklow at Lugnaquillia Mountain summit

23. COUNTY
WEXFORD

Wexford is a coastal county in the southeast corner of Ireland. With an area of 2,353km², it is the thirteenth largest county in Ireland and the largest in Leinster. It shares land boundaries with three other counties: Kilkenny, Carlow and Wicklow.

Notable Geographical Facts about Wexford

Wexford is number 7 on the Irish county height rankings.
It is the most southerly county in Leinster.
Ireland's longest beach is in Wexford. It is the 20km stretch of sand running between Cahore Point and The Raven Point. This includes Morriscastle Beach and Ballinesker Beach.

MOUNT LEINSTER

The trig pillar on Mount Leinster summit marks the shared CHP of Wexford and neighbouring Carlow. Refer to Chapter 23 – County Carlow – for information about Mount Leinster and its walking route description.
The highest unshared summit lying entirely within Wexford is that of Mount Leinster East Top at **S:844:528**. Its 654m summit is located in the Blackstairs Mountains 1.8 km to the east of the CHP.

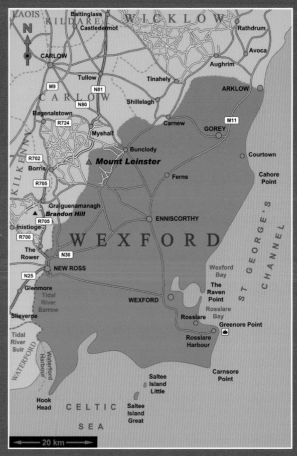

County Wexford

23. COUNTY
CARLOW

Carlow is a landlocked county in the southeast of Ireland. With an area of 896km², it is the thirty-first largest county in Ireland and the eleventh largest in Leinster. It shares boundaries with five other counties: Kildare, Wicklow, Wexford, Kilkenny and Laois.

Notable Geographical Facts about Carlow

Carlow is number 8 on the Irish county height rankings.

The County Low Point of Carlow is at an elevation of approximately 2m above mean sea level, on the county boundary 3km south-southeast of Saint Mullin's where the Pollymounty River joins the tidal River Barrow and leaves Carlow at **S:737:352**.

Carlow has a county height of 793m.

The highest unshared summit lying entirely within Carlow is that of Knockroe at **S:820:496**. Its 540m summit is located 3.1km to the south-southwest of the CHP.

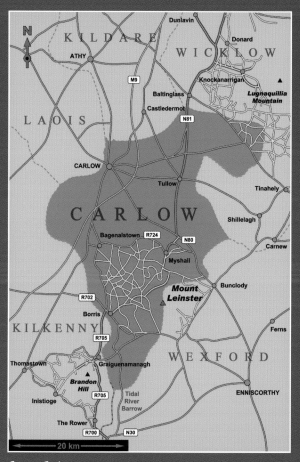

County Carlow

MOUNT LEINSTER

The trig pillar on the stone cairn at the 795m summit of Mount Leinster marks the shared CHP of Wexford and Carlow at **S:827:525**. The summit area is dominated by a large RTÉ NL transmitter site. This summit in the Blackstairs Mountains is classed as a Hewitt, a Marilyn and a Vandeleur-Lynam.

Mount Leinster summit is 9.5km west-southwest of Bunclody, 9.9km east-northeast of Borris and 14.7km northeast of Graiguenamanagh. Any of these locations would make a suitable base for exploring Mount Leinster, the Blackstairs Mountains and the surrounding area.

Route Summary

A straightforward out-and-back walk along the RTÉ NL access road leading to the large telecommunications mast at Mount Leinster summit. The route has a gentle incline – moderate in places – and the CHP is clearly marked by a trig pillar on a stone cairn located to the western side of the compound and outside its perimeter fence. It is best to avoid this summit during wintry conditions due to the risk of ice falling from the mast and its guy wires. An alternative descent and an extension to the nearby summit of Slievebawn are also described.

Time: 1½ to 2¾ hours *Distance:* 5.4km
Ascent: 360m *Grading:* Moderate
Access Restrictions: RTÉ NL access road
Map: OSi Sheet 68.

Start/Finish: the Nine Stones car park at **S:817:546**, 2.3km north-northwest of the CHP. There is space for over thirty cars. Do not block the gated entrance to the RTÉ NL access road. Do not enter the access road with a motor vehicle even if the gate and barrier are open. In-car satnav coordinates for the Nine Stones car park are: (a) **N52°38'12.89", W6°47'37.35"** or (b) **N52.636914°, W6.793708°**.

Route Description

(1) Car park at the Nine Stones (S:81716:54606:437)

Cross the road from the car park and pass through the gap beside the barrier and gate to enter the access road. Follow the road uphill and out of the forest. Arrive at a side track to the left above the forest.

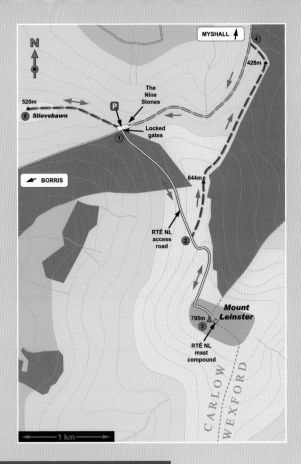

(2) Side track from access road (S:82482:53422:619)

Note the location of this side track as it marks the start of the alternative descent route described below. Continue along the tarmac road for now. On the final straight section leading towards the RTÉ NL compound gate, veer off the road to the right. Continue approximately south to arrive at the trig pillar – the shared CHP of Carlow and Wexford.

(3) Mount Leinster summit (S:82658:52539:795)

Head northwards to rejoin the tarmac. Return to (1) by retracing your steps back down along the access road.

Option A: Alternative descent from (2) to (1)

From (2) on the descent, take the stony path off to the right. Follow this towards the north-northeast. The path become less stony as it approaches the 644m summit. Pass over this summit and continue straight for a short distance. Veer right towards the northeast to follow a fence along a forest boundary fence

Trig pillar marking the shared County High Point of Carlow and Wexford at Mount Leinster summit

on the right. Keep this forest on your right by following a clear path along its perimeter to meet the road.

(4) Path meets road (S:83146:55544:364)

Turn right along the road and follow to arrive at (I).

Option A adds 2.9km of horizontal distance and up to 80 minutes to the descent. It also increases the vertical ascent by 100m.

Option B: Out-and-back extension to Slievebawn summit

From (I), ascend along the broad ridge behind the car park towards the west-northwest. Follow a clear path to arrive at the summit cairn.

(5) Slievebawn summit (S:80650:54811:520)

Return to (I) by retracing your steps.

Option B adds 2.3km of horizontal distance and up to 60 minutes to the route. It also increases the vertical ascent by 90m.

Mount Leinster viewed from the ridge leading to Slievebawn

24. COUNTY
DUBLIN

Dublin is a coastal county in the east of Ireland. With an area of 921km², it is the thirtieth largest county in Ireland and the tenth largest in Leinster. It shares land boundaries with three other counties: Wicklow, Kildare and Meath.

Notable Geographical Facts about Dublin

Dublin is number 10 on the Irish county height rankings.

Based on the latitude/longitude referencing system, Dublin is the most easterly county in the Republic of Ireland. The easternmost point in the Republic is The Nose on Lambay Island at **O:331:512.** (However, based on the distorted Irish Grid system, the easternmost point in the Republic is Wicklow Head at **T:345:924** in neighbouring Wicklow.)

The highest unshared summit lying entirely within Dublin is that of Seahan at **O:081:197**. Its 648m summit is located in the Wicklow Mountains 5.5km to the northwest of the CHP.

County Dublin

KIPPURE

The trig pillar at the 757m summit of Kippure marks the CHP of Dublin at **O:116:155**. The summit area is dominated by a large RTÉ NL transmitter site. This summit in the Wicklow Mountains is classed as a Hewitt, a Marilyn and a Vandeleur-Lynam.

Kippure summit is 10.8km west of Enniskerry, 13.6km east of Blessington and 19.1km south-southwest of Dublin city centre. Any of these locations would make a suitable base for exploring Kippure, the Wicklow Mountains and the surrounding area.

Route Summary

A straightforward out-and-back walk along the RTÉ NL access road leading to the large telecommunications mast at Kippure summit. The route has a gentle incline – moderate in places – and the CHP is clearly marked by a trig pillar located to the northern side of the compound and outside its perimeter fence. It is best to avoid this summit during wintry conditions due to the risk of ice falling from the mast and its guy wires. The route is entirely in Wicklow until reaching the trig pillar. An alternative ascent via Lough Bray Upper is also described.

Time: 1¾ to 3 hours   **Distance:** 7.3km
Ascent: 240m   **Grading:** Moderate
Access Restrictions: RTÉ NL access road
Maps: OSi Sheet 50; Harvey Superwalker *Wicklow Mountains*;
EastWest Mapping *The Dublin & North Wicklow Mountains*.

Start/Finish: at the gated entrance to the RTÉ NL access road on the R115 at **O:141:142**. This is 2.9km east-southeast of the CHP. It is possible to park on either side of the access road's gated entrance without becoming an obstruction. Do not enter the access road with a motor vehicle even if the gate and barrier are open. In-car satnav coordinates for the RTÉ NL access road entrance are: (a) **N53°09'57.98", W6°17'39.74"** or (b) **N53.166106°, W6.294372°**.

Route Description

(1) Gated entrance to RTÉ NL access road (O:14120:14175:521)

Pass through the gap on either side of the locked barrier to enter the access road. Follow the road uphill to where it meets the locked gate of the RTÉ NL compound. Follow the perimeter fence of the compound in either direction to arrive at the trig pillar – the CHP of Dublin.

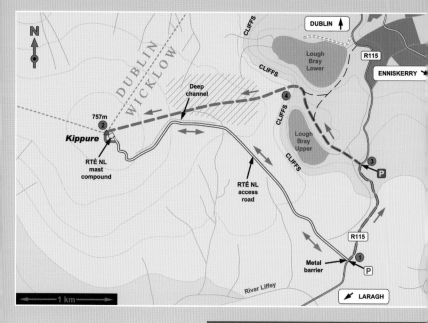

Kippure viewed from road near start point

(2) Summit of Kippure (O:11570:15465:757)

Return to (1) by retracing your steps back down along the access road.

Option A: Alternative ascent from (1) to (2) via Lough Bray Upper

From the start/finish, turn left along the R115 northeast. Follow the road for 1.1km – beware of possible fast-moving traffic along this road. Arrive at a small roadside car park overlooking Lough Bray Upper.

(3) Car park overlooking Lough Bray Upper (O:14228:15132:465)

This car park can easily be used as an alternative start/finish. Turn left off the road here. Descend northwest along a worn path towards Lough Bray Upper. With the lough on your left, follow the high line of a small ridge. Ignore paths leading off to the right. Arrive at the base of a steep, grassy climb approximately midway between the upper and lower loughs. Ascend carefully to the top of the cliff.

(4) Cliff top overlooking Lough Bray Lower (O:13417:15892:568)

Continue west-southwest across rough terrain, which may be boggy in places. In clear visibility, the large mast on Kippure acts as a useful guide until the mountain itself comes into view. In poor visibility, follow a grid bearing of 256° for approximately 2km. Do not be tempted to join the RTÉ NL access road – a deep excavated channel runs alongside the road and is not safe to cross. Maintain a straight line towards the summit. Find an easy route through some peat banks to arrive at the RTÉ NL compound. Approach the fence and turn right along it. Follow the perimeter to arrive at the trig pillar.

Option A adds 1km of horizontal distance and up to forty-five minutes to the ascent. It also increases the vertical ascent by 100m.

Trig pillar marking the County High Point of Dublin at Kippure summit

25. COUNTY
LOUTH

Louth is a coastal county in the northeast of Ireland. With an area of 821km², it is the smallest county in Ireland. It shares land boundaries with three other counties: Meath, Monaghan and Armagh.

Notable Geographical Facts about Louth

Louth is number 20 on the Irish county height rankings.

It is the most northerly county in Leinster. The northernmost point in Leinster is on the Louth-Armagh boundary at **J:080:196**. This is 2.1km north-northeast of the village of Jonesborough.

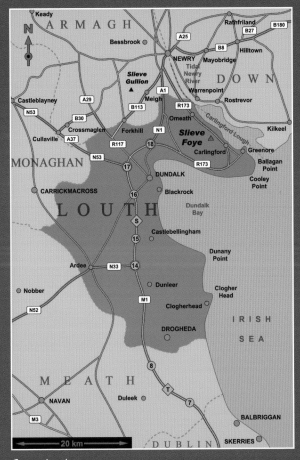

County Louth

SLIEVE FOYE

The trig pillar at the 589m summit of Slieve Foye marks the CHP of Louth at **J:169:119**. This summit in the Cooley Mountains is classed as a Marilyn. It has the added distinctions of being the most northerly and the most easterly CHP in Leinster.

Slieve Foye summit is 2km west of Carlingford, 5.7km south-southeast of Omeath and 11.9km east-northeast of Dundalk. Any of these locations would make a suitable base for exploring Slieve Foye, the Cooley Mountains and the surrounding area.

Route Summary

This out-and-back route starts and finishes at sea level in the historic coastal town of Carlingford. Initially through the streets of the town, the route proceeds along walled paths leading onto the open mountainside. A clear trail leads to a path through rocky terrain around the summit. An extension to Barnavave (Queen Maeve's Gap) is also described.

Walled path through grazing land

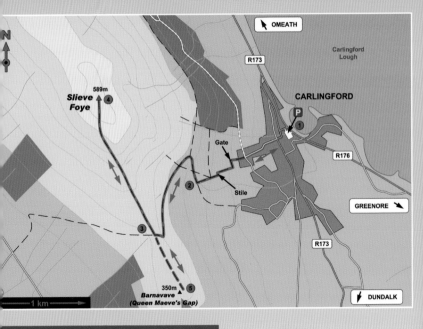

Slieve Foye

Time: 2½ to 4 hours **Distance:** 8.2km
Ascent: 585m **Grading:** Moderate
Access Restrictions: None **Maps:** OSi Sheet 36; OSNI Sheet 29.

Start/Finish: the car park beside Carlingford Tourist Office at **J:189:117,** 2km east of the CHP. There are public toilets beside the car park and easy access to shops, pubs and restaurants in Carlingford. In-car satnav coordinates for the start/finish are: (a) **N54°02'25.94", W6°11'06.39"** or (b) **N54.040539°, W6.185108°**.

Route Description
(1) Car park at Carlingford Tourist Office (J:18944:11666:005)
Walk towards the north exit of the car park. Turn left along the one-way street. Go straight through a crossroads and pass a castle on the right. Arrive at a T-junction where a supermarket is located directly ahead. Turn left here and follow the street south. Turn right at the next junction and follow the street west. Keep on the right-hand side of this street. Keep straight at the next junction. Follow this road uphill to arrive at a crossroads. Take the waymarked path straight ahead. The path becomes narrow between walls and vegetation. Pass through a gate along the way to arrive at a stile. Cross the stile to enter open mountain land and turn right towards west-southwest. Continue straight where the fence turns right. Arrive at a junction of grassy paths.

Trig pillar marking the County High Point of Louth at Slieve Foye summit

(2) Path junction (J:17968:11195:167)

Turn right along the path heading north. The path rises to a junction where it bends sharply to the left. Follow the path left here. Keep along the main path and avoid all minor turn-offs. Arrive at a broad col.

(3) Col between Slieve Foye and Barnavave (J:17513:10651:305)

Turn right and follow a clear path north-northwest. Arrive at the base of a wide gully which presents no obstacle. Follow a clear path through it. At the top of this gully, a waymarker points off to the right. Ignore this, and keep straight instead along a faint trail northwards. In clear visibility, the trig pillar can be seen on the skyline directly ahead. Follow a faint path all the way to the rock-mounted trig pillar – the CHP of Louth.

(4) Slieve Foye summit (J:16903:11935:589)

Retrace your steps to (1).

OPTION A: Out-and-back extension to Barnavave from (3)

From (3), head south-southeast along a faint grassy trail. Keep parallel to a fence on the right. Arrive at the trig pillar on Barnavave.

(5) Barnavave trig pillar (J:17797:10157:358)

Return to (3) by retracing your steps for the outward section of the route.

Option A adds 1.3km of horizontal distance and up to 30 minutes to the route. It also increases the vertical ascent by 50m.

Slieve Foye viewed from Queen Maeve's Gap (Barnavave)

26. COUNTY
LAOIS

Laois is a landlocked county in the south midlands of Ireland. With an area of 1,719km², it is the twenty-fourth largest county in Ireland and the seventh largest in Leinster. It shares boundaries with five other counties: Offaly, Kildare, Carlow, Kilkenny and Tipperary.

Notable Geographical Facts about Laois

Laois is number 24 on the Irish county height rankings.

The County Low Point of Laois is approximately 43m above mean sea level. This is on the county boundary 4km southwest of Carlow town where the River Barrow leaves Laois and enters Carlow at **S:698:736**. Laois has a county height of 484m.

Having no neighbouring coastal counties, Laois is the only double-landlocked county in Ireland. It is, therefore, referred to by some as 'the most landlocked county in Ireland'.

ARDERIN

Two separate points on Arderin represent the CHPs of Laois and neighbouring Offaly. Refer to Chapter 27 – County Offaly – for information about Arderin and its walking route description.

The highest unshared summit lying entirely within Laois is that of Baunreaghcong at **N:326:037**. Its 509m summit is located in the Slieve Bloom Mountains 10.5km to the east-northeast of the CHP.

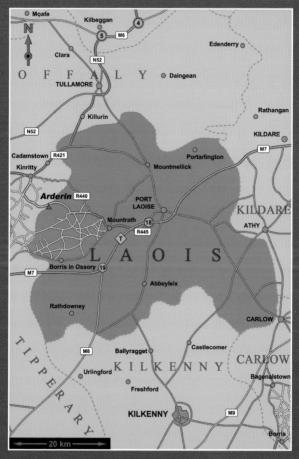

County Laois

27. COUNTY
OFFALY

Offaly is a landlocked county in the south midlands of Ireland. With an area of 2,001km², it is the eighteenth largest county in Ireland and the fifth largest in Leinster. It shares boundaries with seven other counties: Westmeath, Meath, Kildare, Laois, Tipperary, Galway and Roscommon.

Notable Geographical Facts about Offaly

Offaly is number 25 on the Irish county height rankings.

The County Low Point of Offaly is approximately 33m above mean sea level.

Offaly has a county height of 494m.

It is the most westerly county in Leinster.

It is the only Leinster county which shares boundaries with both the neighbouring provinces of Munster and Connacht.

It is worth noting that the highest unshared summit lying entirely within Offaly is that of Stillbrook Hill at **N:261:030**. Its 514m summit is located 5km to the northeast of the CHP.

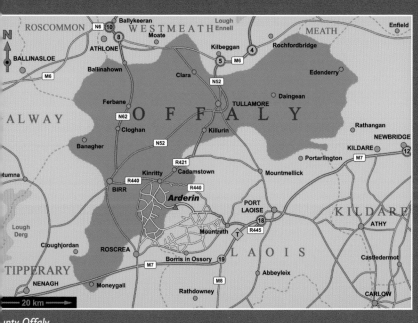

County Offaly

ARDERIN

The ground-level survey marker near the 527m summit of Arderin marks the CHP of Offaly at **S:23234:98901:527**. This is located on the Offaly/Laois boundary approximately 3m west-northwest of the stone cairn. The actual summit of Arderin lies in Laois at an unmarked location approximately 12m east-northeast of the stone cairn and about half a metre higher than it. This actual summit at **S:23247:98907:527** is the CHP of Laois. Arderin summit in the Slieve Bloom Mountains is classed as a Marilyn.

Arderin summit is 12.8km west-northwest of Mountrath and 13.9km northeast of Roscrea. Either of these locations would make a suitable base for exploring Arderin, the Slieve Bloom Mountains and the surrounding area.

Arderin viewed from Glendine Gap

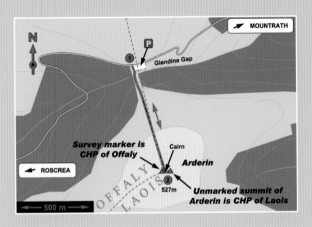

N MOUNTRATH

① Glendine Gap

Survey marker is CHP of Offaly

Cairn

◄ ROSCREA

Arderin

527m

Unmarked summit of Arderin is CHP of Laois

OFFALY LAOIS

◄— 500 m —►

Route Summary

This easy out-and-back route crosses some very boggy ground at the start, but conditions improve on approach to the summit area. It is recommended to walk this route after a period of dry weather.

Time: ½ to 1 hour *Distance:* 1.6km
Ascent: 120m *Grading:* Easy
Access Restrictions: None identified
Map: OSi Sheet 54.

Start/Finish: at Glendine Gap on the Offaly/Laois boundary where there is a car park at **S:230:996**. This is 0.7km north-northwest of the CHPs. In-car satnav coordinates for Glendine Gap are: (a) **N53°02'49.01", W7°39'25.54"** or (b) **N53.046947°, W7.657094°**.

Route Description

(1) Car park at Glendine Gap (S:23047:99609:451)

Stand at the car park entrance and face south-southeast towards Arderin summit. To your right, just beside the car park entrance, a path passes through a shallow cutting. Take this path south-southeast. Make a short pathless descent into a boggy area and ascend the other side to pick up an obvious path. Follow this all the way up to the cairn. Locate the ground-level survey marker just west-northwest of the cairn – the CHP of Offaly. From the cairn, walk 12m towards the east-northeast to locate the actual summit of Arderin – the unmarked CHP of Laois.

(2) Arderin summit (S:23247:98907:527)
Retrace your steps to (1).

Arderin trig point (foreground), cairn, and unmarked summit (middle left)

28. COUNTY
KILKENNY

Kilkenny is a landlocked county in the southeast of Ireland. With an area of 2,062km², it is the sixteenth largest county in Ireland and the third largest in Leinster. It shares boundaries with five other counties: Laois, Carlow, Wexford, Waterford and Tipperary.

Notable Geographical Facts about Kilkenny

Kilkenny is number 26 on the Irish county height rankings.
The County Low Point of Kilkenny is at sea level along the estuaries of the Suir and Barrow rivers which form the county's boundaries with Waterford and Wexford respectively. As its County Low Point experiences the full tidal range, it is debatable that Kilkenny should be classed as a coastal county.

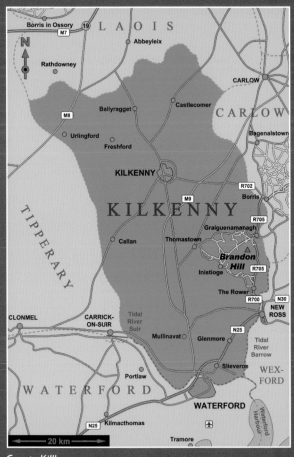

County Killkenny

BRANDON HILL

The trig pillar on top of the stone cairn at the 515m summit of Brandon Hill marks the CHP of Kilkenny at **S:697:403**. The summit area is also furnished with a large cross, a small concrete building and an orientation panel identifying various places which may be visible from the summit, depending on the weather conditions. This summit is classed as a Marilyn and has the added distinction of being the most southerly CHP in Leinster.

Brandon Hill summit is 3.7km south-southwest of Graiguenamanagh, 6.7km east-northeast of Inistioge and 12.8km north of New Ross. Any of these locations would make a suitable base for exploring Brandon Hill and the surrounding area.

Route Summary

This out-and-back route starts along forest tracks leading to clear paths on higher ground. Some steep sections, but ground conditions are generally good. Navigation may be required when descending from the summit. An alternative descent route is also described.

Brandon Hill viewed from the northwest

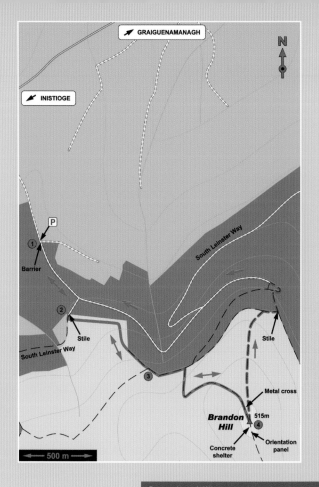

Time: 1½ to 2½ hours **Distance:** 5.3km
Ascent: 300m **Grading:** Moderate
Access Restrictions: None identified **Map:** OSi Sheet 68.

Start/Finish: on a farm track at **S:682:415** where there is a small parking area for up to four cars at the entrance to the Coillte forest, 1.9km northwest of the CHP. The farm track is accessed from **S:678:423** along the main road between Graiguenamanagh and Inistioge. In-car satnav coordinates for the farm track entrance are: (a) **N52°31'40.95", W7°00'08.13"** or (b) **N52.528042°, W7.002258°**.

Track leading towards Brandon Hill summit

Route Description

(1) Start point (S:68229:41461:217)
From the car parking area, take the forest track leading south-southeast. Pass the metal barrier and follow the track to the first junction. Take a right here, and follow to arrive at a gate with a concrete stile beside it.

(2) Stile at forest perimeter (S:68450:41018:251)
Use the concrete stile beside the gate to enter a field. Turn left immediately to follow the edge of the forest eastwards. Arrive at a corner. Turn right uphill to follow the forest boundary southwards. Join a stony path. Follow this southeast along the forest edge to meet a path coming in from the right.

(3) Path junction (S:68996:40607:366)
Keep straight and follow the path along the forest boundary. The path bends left. Take the next path on the right. Follow this southwards initially, then east curving south. Pass a large metal cross on your left. Arrive at the cairn and trig pillar – the CHP of Kilkenny.

(4) Brandon Hill summit (S:69703:40276:515)

Retrace your steps to (I). Descend from the summit along the path to the left of the large metal cross.

Option A: Alternative descent from (4) to (I)

From (4), descend north along the path to the right of the large metal cross. Follow this to intercept a stony path along the forest boundary. Turn right along this for a short distance to arrive at another junction where there is a gate and a metal stile. Turn left and cross the stile. Follow the path downhill towards the south and into the forest. Ignore a minor path on the left. Follow the main path right, then left to arrive at a gravelled turning area. Follow the forest track westwards. At the next junction, take the track on the left. The forest track curves right and descends to meet a track coming in from the left (you passed this point on the ascent). Keep straight here, and follow track to the barrier at the start/finish.

Option A adds 0.9km of horizontal distance and up to 30 minutes to the descent. It does not affect the vertical ascent.

The summit area of Brandon Hill. The trig pillar marks the County High Point of Kilkenny

29. COUNTY
KILDARE

Kildare is a landlocked county in the southeast midlands of Ireland. With an area of 1,694km², it is the twenty-fifth largest county in Ireland and the eighth largest in Leinster. It shares boundaries with six other counties: Meath, Dublin, Wicklow, Carlow, Laois and Offaly.

Notable Geographical Facts about Kildare

Kildare is number 28 on the Irish Irish county height rankings.
The County Low Point of Kildare is approximately 28m above mean sea level.
Kildare has a county height of 351m.
The geographical centre of Leinster **(N:645:073)** is in Kildare, 3.4km south-southeast of Monasterevin.

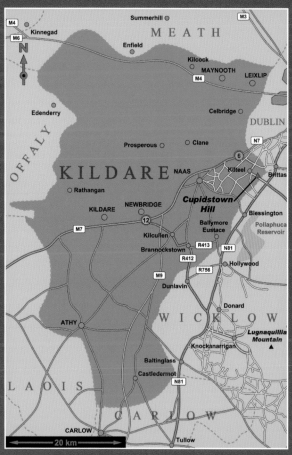

County Kildare

CUPIDSTOWN HILL

The trig pillar at the 379m summit of Cupidstown Hill marks the CHP of Kildare in a field at **O:006:206**. A telecommunications mast is located close to the trig pillar.

Cupidstown Hill summit is 2.2km east-southeast of Kilteel, 2.9km west-southwest of Brittas and 7.1km north-northeast of Blessington. Any of these locations would make a suitable base for exploring Cupidstown Hill and the surrounding area.

Route Summary

This is a straightforward out-and-back stroll along a forest track which leads to a small telecommunications mast at the summit. The route is almost flat, but requires climbing over a locked gate. The CHP is clearly marked by a trig pillar on the edge of a field just beyond the forest perimeter fence, but there is no stile.

Gated forest entrance at the start point

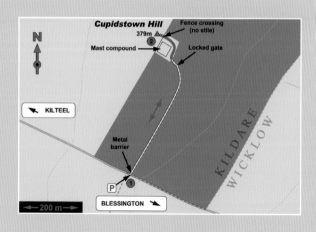

Time: Up to 30 minutes **Distance:** 1.1km
Ascent: 30m **Grading:** Easy
Access Restrictions: None identified, although a locked gate is
encountered along the route and access to the trig pillar involves climbing
over a wire fence
Map: OSi Sheet 50.

Start/Finish: at the entrance to a forest track at **O:005:201**, 480m south-
southwest of the CHP. It is possible to park beside the minor public road at
the forest track entrance. Do not block access to the forest track. In-car
satnav coordinates for the forest track entrance are: (a) **N53°13'20.49",
W6°29'46.61"** or (b) **N53.222358°, W6.496281°**.

Route Description
(1) Entrance to forest track (O:00486:20132:352)
Begin the walk by squeezing through the gap at either end of the yellow and black
metal barrier which spans the entrance to the forest track. Proceed northeast
along the forest track. The track bends to the left. Arrive at a gate. If the gate is
locked, climb over it at the hinged end. Continue along the track to arrive at a
fenced compound containing a telecommunications mast and substation. Walk

past the compound on its right-hand side. The trig pillar becomes visible straight ahead in the field just beyond a wire fence to the northwest. Find a sturdy post and cross the wire fence to enter the field. Cross a dry ditch to arrive at the trig pillar – the CHP of Kildare.

(2) Summit of Cupidstown Hill (O:00586:20604:379)

Return to (1) by retracing your steps along the forest track.

Looking across Kildare from its County High Point

30. COUNTY
LONGFORD

Longford is a landlocked county in the midlands of Ireland. With an area of 1,091km², it is the twenty-ninth largest county in Ireland and the ninth largest in Leinster. It shares boundaries with four other counties: Westmeath, Roscommon, Leitrim and Cavan.

Notable Geographical Facts about Longford
Longford is number 30 on the Irish county height rankings.
The County Low Point of Longford is approximately 35m above mean sea level (the highest County Low Point in Ireland). Longford has a county height of 243m.

County Longford

CORN HILL

The trig pillar on top of the large grass-covered cairn at the 278m summit of Corn Hill marks the CHP of Longford at **N:188:842**. The summit area is dominated by a large RTÉ NL transmitter site and a coniferous forest. This summit is classed as a Marilyn and is most westerly CHP in Leinster. Corn Hill is sometimes referred to as 'Carn Clonhugh' and 'Cairn Hill'.

Corn Hill summit is 3.8km east-southeast of Drumlish, 5.2km northwest of Ballinalee and 10.3km north-northeast of Longford. Any of these locations would make a suitable base for exploring Corn Hill and the surrounding area.

Corn Hill viewed from the northeast

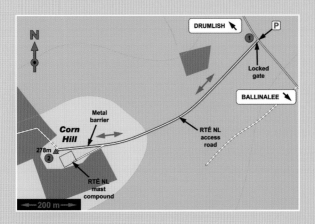

Route Summary

A straightforward out-and-back walk along the RTÉ NL access road leading to the large telecommunications mast on Corn Hill summit. The route has a gentle incline and the CHP is clearly marked by a trig pillar on a grass-covered cairn located to the west of the compound and outside its perimeter fence. It is best to avoid this summit during wintry conditions due to the risk of ice falling from the mast and its guy wires.

Time: Up to ¾ hour **Distance:** 1.8km
Ascent: 60m **Grading:** Easy
Access Restrictions: RTÉ NL access road
Map: OSi Sheet 41.

Start/Finish: at the gated entrance to the RTÉ NL access road at **N:195:846**. This is 840m east-northeast of the CHP. There is a space on the verge for a car to park beside the public road on the north side of the entrance. Do not block the gated entrance to the access road. Do not enter the access road with a motor vehicle even if the gate is open. In-car satnav coordinates for the RTÉ NL access road entrance are: (a) **N53°48'38.43", W7°42'16.97"** or (b) **N53.810675°, W7.704714°**.

Route Description

(1) Gated entrance to RTÉ NL access road (N:19501:84596:218)

Pass through the gap on the right-hand side of the locked gate or use the concrete stile on the left to enter the access road. Follow the road uphill to where it splits near the summit. Keep straight here by taking the track on the right. After a short distance, pass through the gap beside a metal barrier and continue to where the track bends right. Keep straight at this bend by leaving the track. The trig pillar becomes visible beside the mast compound. Ascend the grass-covered cairn to arrive at the trig pillar – the CHP of Longford.

(2) Summit of Corn Hill (N:18756:84215:278)

Retrace your steps to (1).

Trig pillar marking the County High Point of Longford at Corn Hill summit

31. COUNTY
MEATH

Meath is a coastal county in the east of Ireland. With an area of 2,343km², it is the fourteenth largest county in Ireland and the second largest in Leinster. It shares land boundaries with seven other counties: Louth, Dublin, Kildare, Offaly, Westmeath, Cavan and Monaghan.

Notable Geographical Facts about Meath
Meath is number 31 on the Irish Irish county height rankings.
Among the coastal counties of Ireland, Meath has the lowest CHP.

County Meath

CARNBANE EAST

The top of the large cairn – known as Cairn T – at the 276m summit of Carnbane East marks the CHP of Meath at **N:586:776**. The gated entrance to a chamber within this cairn is usually kept locked, but is opened for the equinox illuminations and during the summer if there is a guide on site (a key is available from nearby Loughcrew Gardens if you want to enter Cairn T at other times). OS maps show a triangulation station at the summit, but there is currently no trig pillar on Carnbane East. There is a patch of concrete in a hole on top of Cairn T matching the dimensions of a trig pillar which may have been dismantled in the past. However, the rounded head of a brass object embedded in the concrete may actually be an alternative style of triangulation point used to avoid any visual intrusion at this heritage site. This summit in the Slieve na Calliagh Hills is classed as a Marilyn. It is the lowest CHP in a coastal county of Ireland. Carnbane East is often referred to as 'Slieve na Calliagh' and sometimes as 'Loughcrew'.

Carnbane East summit is 4.3km southeast of Oldcastle, 14.9km north of Delvin and 15.4km west of Kells. Any of these locations would make a suitable base for exploring Carnbane East and the surrounding area.

Carnbane East viewed from the southeast

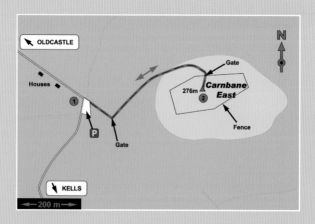

Route Summary

This short out-and-back walk route starts along some steps and a gravel path before following a waymarked path through a green field. It is best to avoid taking dogs on this walk as there may be sheep grazing. The CHP is clearly marked by an obvious stone cairn known as Cairn T.

Time: Up to 30 minutes *Distance:* 1.2km
Ascent: 75m *Grading:* Easy
Access Restrictions: None *Map:* OSi Sheet 42.

Start/Finish: the car park at the Loughcrew Megalithic Graves at **N:582:775,** 420m west of the CHP. In-car satnav coordinates for the start/finish are: (a) **N53°44'39.11", W7°07'07.44"** or (b) **N53.744197°, W7.118733°**.

Route Description

(1) Car park at Loughcrew Megalithic Graves (N:58194:77517:203)

At the northern end of the car park, pass through the black metal bars to access the path. Follow the steps uphill towards the southeast to arrive at a small gate. Pass through the gate to enter a field, and turn left immediately. Some posts mark

Carnbane East start point

the path northeast through the field. Follow these. The path gradually curves uphill to arrive at another small gate. Enter the fenced enclosure through the gate and head south towards Cairn T. Proceed to the top of the cairn – the CHP of Meath.

(2) Summit of Carnbane East (N:58617:77580:276)

Retrace your steps to (1) along the outward section of the route.

Cairn T (in the background) marks the County High Point of Meath at Carnbane East summit

32. COUNTY
WESTMEATH

Westmeath is a landlocked county in the midlands of Ireland. With an area of 1,839km² it is the twenty-first largest county in Ireland and the sixth largest in Leinster. It shares boundaries with five other counties: Meath, Offaly, Longford, Roscommon and Cavan.

Notable Geographical Facts about Westmeath

Westmeath is number 32 on the Irish county height rankings. It has the lowest CHP in Ireland.

The County Low Point is approximately 34m above mean sea level.

Westmeath has a county height of 227m – the smallest in Ireland.

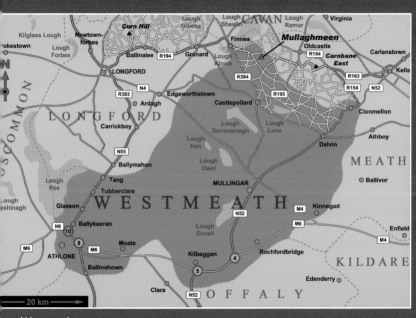

nty Westmeath

MULLAGHMEEN

The stone cairn at the 258m summit of Mullaghmeen marks the CHP of Westmeath at **N:469:794**. The summit area is completely surrounded by Mullaghmeen Forest (reputed to be the largest beech forest in Western Europe), although the views are generally unobstructed in all directions. This summit is classed as a Marilyn and is the lowest CHP in Ireland.

Mullaghmeen summit is 8.3km west of Oldcastle, 9.2km north of Castlepollard and 13.7km east of Granard. Any of these locations would make a suitable base for exploring Mullaghmeen and the surrounding area.

Route Summary

This circular route is entirely along clear tracks and paths through Mullaghmeen Forest Park. For parts, it follows the 'Red' and 'White' waymarked trails.

Mullaghmeen viewed from the northwest

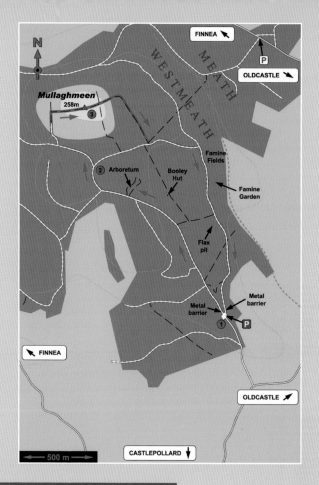

Mullaghmeen

Time: ¾ to 1¾ hour **Distance:** 4.6km
Ascent: 100m **Grading:** Easy
Access Restrictions: None **Map:** OSi Sheet 41.

Start/Finish: Mullaghmeen Forest car park at **N:480:779**, 1.8km southeast of the CHP. Access to the car park is via the forest's main entrance along the minor road at **N:482:774**. In-car satnav coordinates for the forest entrance are: (a) **N53°44'39.87", W7°16'13.72"** or (b) **N53.744408°, W7.270478°**.

Route Description

(1) Mullaghmeen Forest car park (N:47952:77911:162)

There are two tracks with metal barriers at the northern end of the car park. Pick the one on the left. Pass through the gap beside it and follow the 'Red' and 'White' waymarked trails. Keep straight along 'Red' at a junction where 'White' deviates to the left. 'White' rejoins at the next junction. Continue straight and past the arboretum on the right. The waymarked trails split again at the next track junction. Follow 'Red' to the right here as it curves northwards. 'White' rejoins again as a path from the left at the next junction. Continue straight here to where the trails split for a third time.

(2) Leave 'Red' route at track junction (N:47023:78956:215)

Take the track on the left to follow 'White' this time. The track curves from north to northwest. Take the next right along a non-waymarked track heading north. This enters an area of the forest which has been cleared. The track becomes a path. At the next junction, take the path on the right. Follow eastwards to arrive at the summit cairn – the CHP of Westmeath.

(3) Summit of Mullaghmeen (N:46927:79379:258)

Continue straight over the summit by following the path eastwards. Keep straight where the path crosses a grassy trail. The path enters the trees and bends right. Follow this as it descends to meet the 'Red' trail along the forest track. Turn left to follow the forest track east to arrive at a T-junction. Turn right along 'Red' and 'White' and follow the track south all the way back to (1).

Cairn marking the County High Point of Westmeath at Mullaghmeen summit

APPENDIX

County High Point Challenges

Each year sees a growing number of Irish walkers and mountaineers set themselves the goal of visiting the highest point in each of the thirty-two counties. Whether this is a personal challenge or a charity fund-raising venture, there is no better reason to visit every county in Ireland.

The following pages highlight all the various challenges based on Ireland's County High Points. For each different CHP Challenge, the respective map illustrates the most efficient order in which to complete the required CHPs. Indicative travel routes on each of the following maps also allow challengers to plan the logistics for all inter-walk sections where motor transport (or bicycle, etc) is required. These routes are also shown in more detail on maps at the beginning of each chapter in this book.

It is recommended that CHP Challenges are either completed in the order shown on the relevant map, or in the exact reverse order to that shown – e.g. the All-Ireland CHP Challenge could start at the summit of Errigal Mountain and finish at the summit of Mweelrea (as shown), or vice versa.

Regardless of which CHP Challenge is being undertaken, or in which order the respective CHPs are being visited along the way, the challenge (and the clock if it is a timed expedition) officially starts when the challenger leaves the first CHP and begins the first descent. The challenge is officially completed when the challenger physically touches the final CHP. The ascent at the start and descent at the finish are never included in timed CHP Challenges.

The All-Ireland CHP Challenge

The goal is to visit the highest point in each of Ireland's thirty-two counties. This challenge can be achieved by undertaking a series of twenty-six walks, all of which are described in this book. The challenger is required to visit twenty-nine CHPs in order to complete the challenge. Clare and Down each have two locations which currently qualify as CHPs – just one in each is required for the purposes of this challenge.

The Munster CHP Challenge

The goal is to visit the highest point in each of Munster's six counties. This challenge can be achieved by undertaking a series of five walks, all of which are described in this book. The challenger is required to visit six CHPs in order to complete the challenge. Clare has two locations which currently qualify as CHPs – just one of these is required for the purposes of this challenge.

The Connacht CHP Challenge

The goal is to visit the highest point in each of Connacht's five counties. This challenge can be achieved by undertaking a series of four walks, all of which are described in this book. The challenger is required to visit five CHPs in order to complete the challenge.

The Ulster CHP Challenge

The goal is to visit the highest point in each of Ulster's nine counties. This challenge can be achieved by undertaking a series of seven walks, all of which are described in this book. The challenger is required to visit seven CHPs in order to complete the challenge. Down has two locations which currently qualify as CHPs – just one of these is required for the purposes of this challenge.

The Leinster CHP Challenge

The goal is to visit the highest point in each of Leinster's twelve counties. This challenge can be achieved by undertaking a series of ten walks, all of which are described in this book. The challenger is required to visit eleven CHPs in order to complete the challenge.

The Republic of Ireland CHP Challenge

The goal is to visit the highest point in each of the Republic's twenty-six counties. This challenge can be achieved by undertaking a series of twenty-two walks, all of which are described in this book. The challenger is required to visit twenty-five CHPs in order to complete the challenge. Clare has two locations which currently qualify as CHPs – just one of these is required for the purposes of this challenge.

The Northern Ireland CHP Challenge

The goal is to visit the highest point in each of Northern Ireland's six counties. This challenge can be achieved by undertaking a series of five walks, all of which are described in this book. The challenger is required to visit five CHPs in order to complete the challenge. Down has two locations which currently qualify as CHPs – just one of these is required for the purposes of this challenge.

The Irish Four Peaks Challenge

The goal is to visit the highest point in each of Ireland's four provinces. The Provincial High Points equate to the CHPs of Kerry, Mayo, Down and Wicklow. This challenge can be achieved by undertaking a series of four walks, all of which are described in this book. The challenger is required to visit the four CHPs in order to complete the challenge. Down has two locations which currently qualify as CHPs – just one of these is required for the purposes of this challenge.

The All-Ireland CHP Challenge

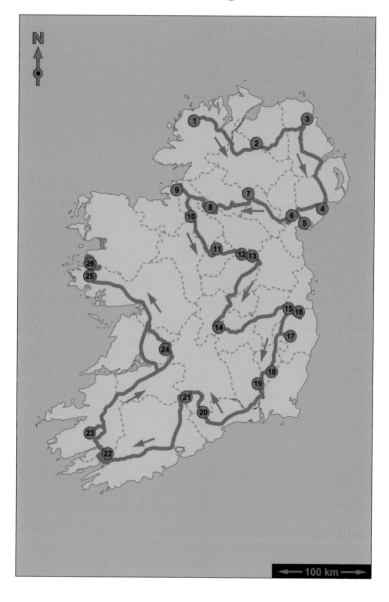

1 Errigal Mountain (chapter 13)
2 Sawel Mountain (chapters 14 and 15)
3 Trostan (chapter 19)
4 Slieve Donard (chapter 12)
5 Slieve Foye (chapter 25)
6 Slieve Gullion (chapter 18)
7 Slieve Beagh East Top (chapter 20)
8 Cuilcagh (chapters 16 and 17)
9 Truskmore (chapters 9 and 10)
10 Seltannasaggart Southeast Slope (chapter 11)
11 Corn Hill (chapter 30)
12 Mullaghmeen (chapter 32)
13 Carnbane East (chapter 31)
14 Arderin (chapters 26 and 27)
15 Cupidstown Hill (chapter 29)
16 Kippure (chapter 24)
17 Lugnaquillia Mountain (chapter 21)
18 Mount Leinster (chapters 22 and 23)
19 Brandon Hill (chapter 28)
20 Knockmealdown (chapter 4)
21 Galtymore Mountain (chapters 2 and 3)
22 Knockboy (chapter 5)
23 Carrauntoohil (chapter 1)
24 Moylussa (chapter 6)
25 Benbaun (chapter 8)
26 Mweelrea (chapter 7)

The Provincial CHP Challenges

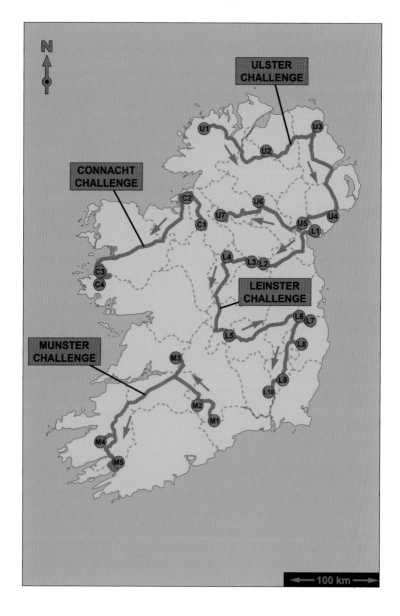

Ulster Challenge

U1 Errigal Mountain (chapter 13)
U2 Sawel Mountain (chapters 14 and 15)
U3 Trostan (chapter 19)
U4 Slieve Donard (chapter 12)
U5 Slieve Gullion (chapter 18)
U6 Slieve Beagh East Top (chapter 20)
U7 Cuilcagh (chapters 16 and 17)

Munster Challenge

M1 Knockmealdown (chapter 4)
M2 Galtymore Mountain (chapters 2 and 3)
M3 Moylussa (chapter 6)
M4 Carrauntoohil (chapter 1)
M5 Knockboy (chapter 5)

Leinster Challenge

L1 Slieve Foye (chapter 25)
L2 Carnbane East (chapter 31)
L3 Mullaghmeen (chapter 32)
L4 Corn Hill (chapter 30)
L5 Arderin (chapters 26 and 27)
L6 Cupidstown Hill (chapter 29)
L7 Kippure (chapter 24)
L8 Lugnaquillia Mountain (chapter 21)
L9 Mount Leinster (chapters 22 and 23)
L10 Brandon Hill (chapter 28)

Connacht Challenge

C1 Seltannasaggart Southeast Slope (chapter 11)
C2 Truskmore (chapters 9 and 10)
C3 Mweelrea (chapter 7)
C4 Benbaun (chapter 8)

The Republic of Ireland CHP Challenge

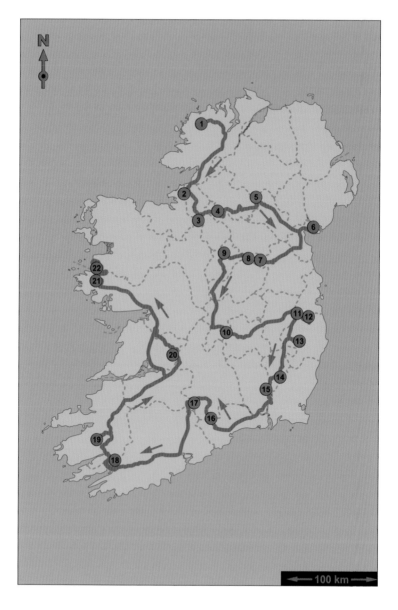

1 Errigal Mountain (chapter 13)
2 Truskmore (chapters 9 and 10)
3 Seltannasaggart Southeast Slope (chapter 11)
4 Cuilcagh (chapters 16 and 17)
5 Slieve Beagh East Top (chapter 20)
6 Slieve Foye (chapter 25)
7 Carnbane East (chapter 31)
8 Mullaghmeen (chapter 32)
9 Corn Hill (chapter 30)
10 Arderin (chapters 26 and 27)
11 Cupidstown Hill (chapter 29)
12 Kippure (chapter 24)
13 Lugnaquillia Mountain (chapter 21)
14 Mount Leinster (chapters 22 and 23)
15 Brandon Hill (chapter 28)
16 Knockmealdown (chapter 4)
17 Galtymore Mountain (chapters 2 and 3)
18 Knockboy (chapter 5)
19 Carrauntoohil (chapter 1)
20 Moylussa (chapter 6)
21 Benbaun (chapter 8)
22 Mweelrea (chapter 7)

The Northern Ireland CHP Challenge

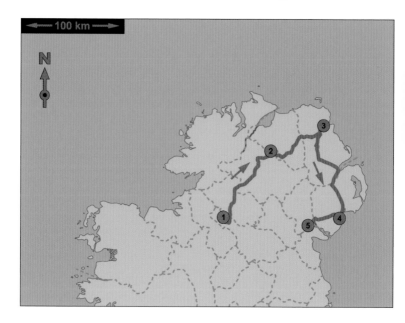

1 Cuilcagh (chapters 16 and 17)

2 Sawel Mountain (chapters 14 and 15)

3 Trostan (chapter 19)

4 Slieve Donard (chapter 12)

5 Slieve Gullion (chapter 18)

The Irish Four Peaks Challenge

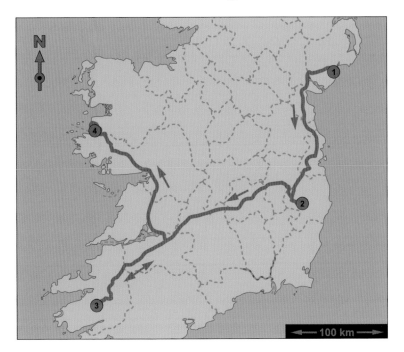

1 Slieve Donard (chapter 12)

2 Lugnaquillia Mountain (chapter 21)

3 Carrauntoohil (chapter 1)

4 Mweelrea (chapter 7)

References & Further Reading

Websites
The Mountainviews website was selected by the author as being the most reliable source of spot height information for County High Points and other prominent summits mentioned throughout this book. www.mountainviews.ie

Maps
All maps referred to while researching this book have been recommended in the respective walking route descriptions.

Walking Guidebooks
Walking in Ireland by Sandra Bardwell, Helen Fairbairn and Gareth McCormack (Lonely Planet Publications)

The Mountains of Ireland by Paddy Dillon (Cicerone)

Northern Ireland – A Walking Guide by Helen Fairbairn (The Collins Press)

The Dingle, Iveragh and Beara Peninsulas – A Walking Guide by Adrian Hendroff (The Collins Press)

Donegal, Sligo & Leitrim – A Walking Guide by Adrian Hendroff (The Collins Press)

Best Irish Walks by Joss Lynam (Gill & Macmillan)

Connemara & Mayo – A Walking Guide by Paul Phelan (The Collins Press)

Carrauntoohil & MacGillycuddy's Reeks: A Walking Guide to Ireland's Highest Mountains by Jim Ryan (The Collins Press)

Tipperary & Waterford – A Walking Guide by John G. O'Dwyer (The Collins Press)

West Cork Walks by Kevin Corcoran (O'Brien Press)

Other Books
The Height of Nonsense by Paul Clements (The Collins Press)

Complete Irish Wildlife by Paul Sterry and Derek Mooney (Harper Collins)

From High Places by Adrian Hendroff (The History Press Ireland)

Glossary

Col – the lowest point on a ridge linking two hills and/or mountains.

County height – the **elevation** gained within a county between its **County Low Point** and **County High Point**.

Geographical centre – for the purposes of this book, the geographical centre is the point within a particular area whose easting coordinate value is the mean average of the area's westernmost and easternmost extreme eastings, and whose northing coordinate value is the mean average of the area's southernmost and northernmost extreme northings.

Hewitt – an acronym-based classification for any (H)ill in (E)ngland, (W)ales or (I)reland whose **summit** is higher than (T)wo (T)housand feet above sea level and having at least a 30m **prominence**.

Irish county height rankings – a numbered list of counties in Ireland based on the **elevation** gained within each county between its **County Low Point** and **County High Point**. On this list, Kerry has the greatest county height, and has the highest ranking of 1. Westmeath has the smallest county height, and has the lowest ranking of 32. Where two coastal counties share the same CHP, the county with the longer coastal length is ranked higher.

Marilyn – a classification for any summit in Ireland or the UK having at least a 150m **prominence** – the one and only requirement for this classification.

Munro – a classification type reserved only for certain Scottish summits higher than 3,000 feet (914.4m) above sea level. There does not appear to be a set **prominence** requirement, but this continues to be debated. The first Munro list was created by Sir Hugh Munro, a Scottish mountaineer, in 1891. There are no Munros in Ireland, although Irish summits meeting the height requirement of 3,000 feet are often referred to as 'Munros', 'Irish Munros' or 'Furth Munros'.

Prominence – the relative height of a summit above the lowest contour within which that particular summit represents the highest point.

Trig pillar – a triangulation station constructed in the form of a small concrete obelisk. Trig pillars exist at hundreds of prominent locations throughout Ireland.

Vandeleur-Lynam – a classification type for any Irish **summit** higher than 600m above sea level and having at least a 15m **prominence**.

Personal Progress Record

COUNTY HEIGHT RANKING	COUNTY	COUNTY HIGH POINT (CHP)	FULL COORDINATES OF COUNTY HIGH POINT	OS 1:50k SHEET	COMPLETION DATE
1	Kerry	CARRAUNTOOHIL	V:80361:84425:1039	78	
2	Wicklow	LUGNAQUILLIA MOUNTAIN	T:03211:91779:925	56	
3	Limerick	GALTYMORE MOUNTAIN (summit cairn)	R:87848:23793:919	74	
4	Tipperary	GALTYMORE MOUNTAIN (broken trig pillar)	R:87851:23795:919	74	
5	Down	SLIEVE DONARD (trig pillar)	J:35789:27687:853	29	
5	Down	SLIEVE DONARD (summit cairn)	J:35802:27693:850	29	
6	Mayo	MWEELREA	L:78977:66813:814	37	
7	Wexford	MOUNT LEINSTER (shared trig pillar)	S:82658:52539:795	68	
8	Carlow				
9	Waterford	KNOCKMEALDOWN	S:05801:08410:794	74	
10	Dublin	KIPPURE	O:11570:15465:757	56	
11	Donegal	ERRIGAL MOUNTAIN	B:92824:20774:751	1	
12	Galway	BENBAUN	L:78556:53904:729	37	
13	Cork	KNOCKBOY	W:00481:62060:706	85	
14	Derry	SAWEL MOUNTAIN (shared trig pillar)	H:61796:97303:678	13	
15	Tyrone				
16	Fermanagh	CUILCAGH (shared trig pillar)	H:12354:28011:665	26	
17	Cavan				
18	Sligo	TRUSKMORE	G:75893:47341:647	16	
19	Leitrim	TRUSKMORE SOUTHEAST SLOPE	G:76312:47096:631	16	
20	Louth	SLIEVE FOYE	J:16903:11935:589	29 or 36	
21	Armagh	SLIEVE GULLION	J:02482:20337:573	29 or 36	
22	Antrim	TROSTAN	D:17960:23596:550	9	
23	Clare	MOYLUSSA (unmarked southeast summit)	R:65115:75573:532	58	
23	Clare	MOYLUSSA (unmarked northwest summit)	R:64835:75928:532	58	
24	Laois	ARDERIN (unmarked summit)	S:23247:98907:527	54	
25	Offaly	ARDERIN (ground-level survey marker)	S:23234:98901:527	54	
26	Kilkenny	BRANDON HILL	S:69703:40276:515	68	
27	Roscommon	SELTANNASAGGART SOUTHEAST SLOPE	G:90414:19521:412	26	
28	Kildare	CUPIDSTOWN HILL	O:00586:20604:379	50	
29	Monaghan	SLIEVE BEAGH EAST TOP	H:53177:43571:373	18 or 28A	
30	Longford	CORN HILL	N:18756:84215:278	34	
31	Meath	CARNBANE EAST	N:58617:77580:276	42	
32	Westmeath	MULLAGHMEEN	N:46927:79379:258	41	

Walking Guides from The Collins Press

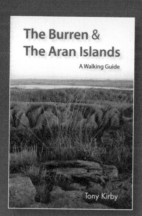

The Burren & The Aran Islands
A Walking Guide

Tony Kirby

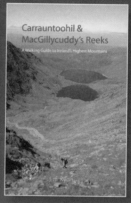

Carrauntoohil & MacGillycuddy's Reeks
A Walking Guide to Ireland's Highest Mountains

Jim Ryan

CONNEMARA & MAYO
Mountain, Coastal & Island Walks
A Walking Guide

Paul Phelan

THE DINGLE, IVERAGH & BEARA PENINSULAS
A Walking Guide

Adrian Hendroff

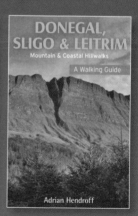

DONEGAL, SLIGO & LEITRIM
Mountain & Coastal Hillwalks
A Walking Guide

Adrian Hendroff